WORKMANSHIP

Honouring the LORD with our Work

Yen Adams

ISBN: 978 – 9988 – 3 – 2947 – 1

Published by;
Graduate Standards Secretarial Services (GS3)
Ayeduase – Kumasi
Tel: +233 249 590 677

Unless otherwise indicated, all scriptural references are taken from the King James Version of the Holy Bible.

DEDICATION

To my lovely wife, Susan, with love.

INTRODUCTION

"For we are labourers together with God: ye are God's husbandry, ye are God's building" **1 Corinthians 3:9**

We are all God's creation but not all of us are His children. As the creation of God, we have been given the freewill to make choices but every choice goes with consequences (**Hebrews 9:27**). We have all sinned against God and have been condemned by the Law to suffer eternal punishment in hell (**Romans 3:23, 6:23**). God is just; He will punish every sin (**Deuteronomy 32:4**). The only payment for sin God will accept is blood (**Hebrews 9:22, Leviticus 17:11**). But God loves us so much, He made a way to pay for our sins. The Bible says He paid fully for all our sins with the blood of His Son Jesus Christ according to **Romans 5:6-9** *"For when we were yet without strength, in due time Christ died for the ungodly. For scarcely for a righteous man will one die: yet peradventure for a good man some would even dare to* *die. But God commendeth his love toward us, in that, while we were yet sinners, Christ died for us. Much more then, being now justified by his blood, we shall be saved from wrath through him"*.

Although the LORD has paid fully for our sins, we must accept the blood of Jesus Christ as full payment for our sins through faith to receive forgiveness of sins and become the Children of God (**John 1:12**). Once we believe on Jesus Christ as our saviour and become the children of God, we are given eternal life (**John 3:16, 3:36, 1 John 5:11-12**) and we shall never lose our salvation (**John 6:37, 10:27-29**). This is the summary of the true Gospel of Jesus Christ (**1 Corinthians 15:1-9**).

The children of God are called believers or Christians. Those who do not believe on Jesus Christ alone as their saviour are called unbelievers. The unbeliever is already condemned and under the wrath of God (**John 3:36**). Unless he repents and accepts Christ's payment for his sins, he will die in his sins and perish in hell (**Psalm 9:17**) regardless of his good works (**Titus 3:5, Ephesians 2:8-9**). Thus, the unbeliever may receive human praise and rewards for his good works on earth but he shall not attract any rewards from the LORD at the judgement seat of Christ and definitely, his good works cannot buy him a place in Heaven (**Ephesians 2:8-9**). There is no single verse in the whole Bible where God promised to reward the good works of unbelievers with eternal life. Heaven cannot be bought with good works.

The believer, on the other hand, is a child of God who returns to his Father in Heaven after death (**1 Thessalonians 4:14**). The LORD has promised to reward the works of the believer at the judgement seat of Christ (**2 Corinthians 5:10, Romans 14:10**). As children of God, the LORD will punish our sins here on earth (**Hebrews 12:6-11, Proverbs 3:12**) but we shall never perish in hell after death (**John 5:24**). However, we are saved to love and serve the LORD (**Ephesians 2:10**). The only way we show our love and appreciation to God for given us His only begotten Son who died for us, is by keeping His commandments (**John 14:15**). He has given us His Word to instruct us and the Holy Spirit to empower and guide us to accomplish His will (**2 Timothy 3:16-17, Acts 1:8**). The first responsibility of the believer is to obey God in every aspect of his life (**1 Timothy 4:12**). The second responsibility of the believer is to tell others about the Gospel. This is called soul-winning, evangelism or the great commission (**Matthew 28:18-20**). Every believer is commanded to win souls. The two must go together. Without the Christian life or good works, we lose the moral grounds and the power required to preach the Gospel effectively. The LORD has promised to bless and reward every believer who serves faithfully (**Mark 10:29-30, Matthew 16:27**).

Honouring God with our Work

Man was created to bring pleasure to God (**Revelations 4:11**). As children of God, the LORD owns us and everything we have (**John 3:27**). He has full authority over our lives. Yet, He has given us the freewill to love and honour Him. If we walk in His full will in any aspect of our lives, He will bless that area and use it to His glory (**John 15:2**). One important aspect of our lives that we often regard as less spiritual is the work we do for a living, our businesses or career jobs. The LORD places very high spiritual importance on our work. The

Bible teaches a lot of principles we can adopt to successfully serve God in our workplaces. Measuring by the standards of the Bible, many of us have failed to honour God in our workplaces. We have been working far below the standards spelt out in the Bible. The reason why most people are not serving right in their workplaces is because they don't know what God requires from them in their work. This book is written for matured believers who have the desire to serve God with their work.

The book deals with time-tested Biblical principles that will help believers understand what God expects of them in the workplace. It is written from an uncompromising Biblical point of view, based solely on the King James Bible (KJV). The book commences by defining the role of works in the life of a believer. The motivation of the believer to work and the principles that should guide him in choosing a career and a place to work are then examined. We proceed to present the attitude required of a believer in the workplace and how we ought to apply ourselves to our jobs. The doctrine and principles of work are validated by examining the life and works of great men of God in the Bible who successfully applied these principles in their duties. We then demonstrate that these time-tested principles are still profitable in today's technology-driven and fast-changing workplace. The overall goal is to exhort believers to fulfil the will of God in their workplaces and bear fruit for the LORD with their work.

I was born in an Islamic home and raised by grandparents who practiced traditional African religion. Like many young people from broken homes, I have lived a foolish and perverse lifestyle as a young person. As a teenager, I believed in the existence of God but I didn't know which God to serve. My father was a Muslim, my grandparents whom I lived with were traditionalists and later my mother became a Christian. This raised many unanswered questions in my mind.

During my second year in high school, I visited a Church with my friends. After a few regular visits I got baptised and stayed in the Charismatic Church for the rest of my time in high school and later joined the Church of Pentecost, where my mother is a member. Still with many unanswered questions, but a desire to know God, I stayed with the Church of Pentecost as a nominal Christian throughout my undergraduate studies at KNUST, Kumasi, Ghana. During my national service as a teaching assistant at KNUST, I was a regular visitor at Calvary Charismatic Centre (CCC) in Kumasi. At this point, I had made up my mind to become a serious Christian after a long process of questioning and scrutinizing my Islamic and traditional heritage. I had developed a strong zeal to serve God. I attended Church programs on and off campus and followed most of the popular preachers and televangelists of the day. I bought and read most of the popular books, listened to their preaching and attended their programs. I was a typical zealous youth in the Charismatic Church who was searching for truth. Although I didn't know the details of Salvation, I strongly believed in Salvation by works because that was all I knew. I believed that my good works will save me from hell. I also believed that I will lose my salvation when I sin until I confess my sins, although I had publicly confessed Jesus Christ as my saviour. This is typical of many professing Christians in Ghana. Unfortunately, this gospel has no sound Biblical standing. If we could earn eternal life with our own works, then we don't need a saviour (**Galatians 2:21**). One only need a saviour if he can't do anything to save himself.

In 2011, I travelled to Norway to pursue graduate studies at the University of Stavanger. I started visiting an Independent Baptist Church close to the university called Faith Baptist Church. I attended the Church for two years without paying detailed attention to the preaching because I was still following my favourite televangelist on YouTube. After my master's studies, I was awarded another full scholarship to pursue a Ph.D. in Petroleum Engineering. This guaranteed me at least four more years in Norway and in the Church. And what a blessing that turned out to be!

When I was about to turn 30, I decided to read through the whole Bible once in a year. That was the turning point of my life. As I read through the Bible, I found so many teachings that contradicted my favourite preachers and a lot of things I thought I knew. I shared my findings with my wife and we approached the Pastor who offered to teach us the Gospel. That was the first time in over ten years of going to Church that The True Gospel was explained to us in a way that the whole Bible made sense and answered most of the questions we had accumulated over the years. I came to truly understand why the Gospel is called "good news". We understood the Gospel, that salvation is only by faith in Jesus Christ who died for us and shed His blood to pay fully for all our sins **(John 3:16, Romans 5:8, 1 John 5:11-12, Ephesians 2:8-9)**. By trusting Him alone as our saviour, we become Children of God who will never lose our salvation **(John 5:24, 6:37, 10:27-29)**. We trusted on Jesus Christ alone as our saviour on 21st April, 2015. Since that day, our passion to study the Word of God and pursue truth has been insatiable. In 2018, we moved back to Ghana to preach the Gospel and share our testimony. Our life verse is **John 6:68** *"Then Simon Peter answered him, Lord, to whom shall we go? thou hast the words of eternal life."*

At the writing of this book, we have been married for more than seven years and the LORD has blessed us immensely with four children; three boys and a girl. Our goal as a family is to preach the Gospel and demonstrate the practicality of the Word of God in our daily lives. We believe that, every Word in the Bible is absolute truth, infallible and profitable. We believe that the Bible is the ultimate authority for faith and practice, and that no person or document can surpass the Bible. We practice the principles presented in this book. We are not perfect at everything but we have practiced them over the years and they have been a huge blessing in our lives. We are Independent Baptists and members of Baptists Bible Study in Kumasi. We are soul-winning Baptists who love the LORD and people. We visit people in their homes with The Gospel of Jesus Christ and preach sound Biblical doctrine in Church. You can reach us with any question about God, the Bible or the Christian faith.

Acknowledgements

All glory to God and our LORD Jesus Christ who have chosen the foolish things of the world to confound the wise, and the weak things of the world to confound the things which are mighty (**1 Corinthians 1:27**). I should be the last person God will consider to use to write a book such as this. I also owe this book to my lovely wife, Susan. What can I do without her? *"Who can find a virtuous woman? for her price is far above rubies"* (**Proverbs 31:10**). I am extremely grateful to Pastor James Turpin and his wife, Ruth, of Faith Baptist Church, Stavanger, Norway, for leading us to the LORD and giving us a foundation in sound Biblical doctrine including the major principles of work presented in this book. I would like to thank Pastor Seth Turpin and his wife Naomi for training and mentoring us. Special thanks to Paul Effah for taking time to read through and edit the manuscript. He has been part of this book right from when the idea was conceived. I would like to thank Pastor Samson Laniran of the Fundamental Independent Baptist Church, Kumasi, for the opportunity to teach some of the principles in this book in his Church. I am thankful to Professor Kwesi Obiri-Danso, former Vice Chancellor of KNUST, for allowing God to use him to provide a job for me as a Lecturer at the Department of Petroleum Engineering, KNUST. Finally, special appreciation goes to Pastor John Sommer of Biblical Baptist Church, Kumasi and Pastor Aaron Andrew of Baptist Bible Study, Kumasi, where we are members, for their teachings, friendship and warm fellowship. They have been such a blessing and encouragement to us, our growth in the faith and transition to Ghana.

Yen Adams Sokama-Neuyam, Ph.D.
Kumasi, Ghana.
Email: yen.adams@hotmail.com

CONTENTS

1. The workmanship of God   1

2. Reasons to work   27

3. Attitude at work   47

4. Men who worked   71

5. Preparing to work   115

6. Getting ahead at work   155

7. Family and work   189

THE WORKMANSHIP OF GOD

"For we are his workmanship, created in Christ Jesus unto good works, which God hath before ordained that we should walk in them." **Ephesians 2:10**

In **Matthew 5:20** Jesus said *"…That except your righteousness shall exceed the righteousness of the scribes and Pharisees, ye shall in no case enter into the kingdom of heaven"*. This is one of the most terrifying statements in the whole Bible. If the righteousness mentioned here means keeping the Law, or ten commandments, then none of us will stand a chance of going to Heaven because it is practically impossible for anyone to keep the law better than the Pharisees and scribes. They learn the whole Law from childhood, and keep it throughout their lives. They fast twice every week and pay tithes on almost everything they have (**Luke 18:12**). In the sight of men, they were the most holy people at the time. Yet, Jesus said this is not enough to take anyone to Heaven.

You are probably doing a lot of good works and hoping it will take you to Heaven. Are you doing better than the scribes and Pharisees? How can we get a righteousness that exceed the righteousness of the scribes and Pharisees?

We learn from the Bible that no man can keep all the commandments of God perfectly (**Romans 3:10, Romans 3:23, 1 John 1:8, 10**). We also learn that all our works of righteousness are like filthy rags in the sight of God (**Isaiah 64:6**). If salvation came by keeping the Law or doing good works, no man will be saved (**Galatians 2:16**). If salvation came by the Law, we wouldn't need a saviour (**Galatians 2:21**). On the other hand, if our works cannot give us eternal life, why was the Ten Commandments given? Why are we commanded to keep all these laws and carry out so many other tasks for God if all our works will not count for salvation? It is very important to understand the place of works in the life of the believer. Before salvation, the law plays a significant role in leading a sinner to repentance.

After salvation, obeying the law and doing works of righteousness builds the testimony of the believer to make him useful for God. But in salvation, the law does not play any role. Obeying the law and doing good works cannot save a man from hell because no man can do enough. There is a better way, a righteousness that exceeds the righteousness of the scribes and Pharisees and that is what Jesus was talking about.

Works Fully Defined

The works of the believer consist of two parts: doing what God has commanded us to do and not doing what God has commanded us not to do. We have been commanded to carry out several works of righteousness or good works (**Ephesians 2:10**). The greatest among them is the Great Commission or Soul Winning. It is a sin to refuse to do the will of God. This is summarized in **James 4:17** as "*Therefore to him that knoweth to do good, and doeth it not, to him it is sin*". Jonah disobeyed God by refusing to go and preach at Nineveh. This kind of disobedience or sin is called omission. The other form of disobedience is when we do something that God has clearly commanded us not to do or breaking the laws and commandments of God (**1 John 3:4**). The standard of the law is summarized in **James 2:10** as *"For whosoever shall keep the whole law, and yet offend in one point, he is guilty of all"*. For example, King David disobeyed God when he killed Uriah the Hittite and married his wife. That form of sin is called commission. Therefore, obeying the ten commandments, even if it was possible, doesn't mean we are doing the complete will of God. The two parts are equally important to God. In total, there are about 90 commandments of God in the book of Ephesians alone that the believer is required to obey. That should be troubling to people who are trying to buy eternal life with their works. How many good works must one do to pay his way into Heaven? It is simply impossible.

Works Before Salvation

We read in **Romans 3:19** *"Now we know that what things soever the law saith, it saith to them who are under the law: that every mouth may be stopped, and all the world may become guilty before God"*. Without the laws and commandments of God, there is no way we can know what is right and wrong in the sight of God (**Romans 3:20**). The ten commandments or the Law show us the full standard required by God. If a man wants to please God, he must know what God requires. The Law was given so that when every man stands before God "*every mouth may be stopped, and all the world may become guilty before God*". The Law makes every sincere man guilty before God. It condemns every man as a sinner, not just a small sinner but a very wicked sinner who deserve nothing but hell.

Before **verse 19**, the Bible tells us how we are doing when measured according to the standards of the Law "*As it is written, There is none righteous, no, not one: There is none that understandeth, there is none that seeketh after God. They are all gone out of the way, they are together become unprofitable; there is none that doeth good, no, not one. Their throat is an open sepulchre; with their tongues they have used deceit; the poison of asps is under their lips: Whose mouth is full of cursing and bitterness: Their feet are swift to shed blood: Destruction and misery are in their ways: And the way of peace have they not known: There is* *no fear of God before their eyes*" (**Romans 3:10-18**). We further read in **Jeremiah 17:9** "*The heart is deceitful above all things, and desperately wicked: who can know it?*". You may say you are not as wicked as these scriptures portray because you only tell small lies. We read in **James 2:10** that "*For whosoever shall keep the whole law, and yet offend in one point, he is guilty of all*". Assuming you've kept the whole Law except that "small lie", in the sight of God, you are actually guilty of breaking all the laws. This should make every sincere man feel horribly condemned when he stands before God. No man can boast before God that he has kept the law fully. This condemnation is the first step to repentance. A man cannot be saved until he knows and accept that he is a wicked and helpless sinner before God. That is exactly what leads to Biblical repentance – sorrow of sin and a change of mind about one's own ability to save himself. But even repentance is the work of the Holy Spirit. He convicts us of sin (**John 16:8**).

Works in Salvation

Salvation simply means being saved from sin or having one's sin paid fully. We read in **Romans 6:23** *"For the wages of sin is death..."*. This scripture tells us that the price for sin or the reward for sin is death. What we owe God for breaking His law is death. Man is made up of three parts: spirit, soul and body (**1 Thessalonians 5:23**). Death defined in this context includes physical death (**Hebrews 9:27**) and spiritual death (**Isaiah 59:2, Revelation 20:14**). Physical death is the separation of the soul and spirit from the body. The soul and spirit returns to God for judgement and the body is buried here on earth. Spiritual death is defined as the separation of man from God and the eventual destruction of his soul in hell and the lake of fire (**Isaiah 59:2, Revelations 20:14**). The debt we owe God for our sins is these two forms of death. If I owe you a huge amount of money and I ask you to accept some good works I have done for other people as payment for the money I owe you, would you accept it? No. Because, I don't owe you good works. I owe you money. Our good works do not count for salvation because they can't pay for our sins. The wages of sin is death, not good works.

Throughout the Old Testament scriptures, God has always required blood as payment for sin. Why blood? Because to get blood, an animal must die. Something must die in place of the sinner to pay for the wages of sin (death). This is the reason for all the sacrifices made in the Old Testament. We read in **Hebrews 9:22** *"And almost all things are by the law purged with blood; and without shedding of blood is no remission"*. In **Leviticus 17:11** we read that *"For the life of the flesh is in the blood: and I have given it to you upon the altar to make an atonement for your souls: for it is the blood that maketh an atonement for the soul"*. In the Old Testament, sin was always paid with the blood of animals. When Adam and Eve sinned, God killed an animal and used the skin to cloth them so they can appear righteous before Him (**Genesis 3:21**). God accepted Abel's blood sacrifice for payment of sins and rejected the fruit offering of Cain (**Genesis 4:1-10**). God provided a lamb as replacement to be sacrificed in place of Isaac on mount Moriah (**Genesis 22:10-13**). The angel of death passed over all houses where the blood of a lamb was painted on the door posts during the first Passover (**Exodus 12:29-30**). This runs throughout the Old Testament. Every form of purification of sin in the Temple required the blood of an animal.

We are told that even these sacrifices could not remove sin according to **Hebrews 10:4** *"For it is not possible that the blood of bulls and of goats should take away sins"*. They were only pointing us to a better sacrifice God was going to provide in the future for the whole world according to **Hebrews 10:1** *"For the law having a shadow of good things to come, and not the very image of the things, can never with those sacrifices which they offered year by year continually make the comers thereunto perfect"*. To pay for our sins, we must either die and serve the punishment of our sin in hell or someone must die for us. Unfortunately, no man can die to pay for the sins of other people because we have all sinned and our blood is cursed and unfit to be used as payment of sin (**Genesis 3, Exodus 12:5, 1 Peter 1:19**).

But God so loved the world that He gave us His only begotten Son, Jesus Christ, who died to pay fully for all our sins with His blood (**John 3:16, Romans 5:8**). We have all sinned against God and the payment for our sin is death. Our sins must be paid with the blood of a spotless lamb, that is perfect blood. No one can provide this payment for his own sin and that made the whole world helpless. God provided a Saviour, Jesus Christ, the perfect lamb who was killed on the cross, shed His perfect blood to make atonement or payment for all our sin. That is summarized in **Romans 5:6-9** *"For when we were yet without strength, in due time Christ died for the ungodly. For scarcely for a righteous man will one die: yet peradventure for a good man some would even dare to die. But God commendeth his love toward us, in that, while we were yet sinners, Christ died for us. Much more then, being now justified by his blood, we shall be saved from wrath through him."* The Bible says the death of Jesus Christ is the full payment for our sins (**1 John 2:2**). Salvation is a completely free gift from God as we read in **Ephesians 2:8-9** *"For by grace are ye saved through faith; and that not of yourselves: it is the gift of God: Not of works, lest any man* should boast". **Titus 3:5** also says *"Not by works of righteousness which we have done, but according to his mercy he saved us, by the washing of regeneration, and renewing of the Holy Ghost;"*. We receive the payment of sin through Jesus Christ by Faith. We read in John **3:14-15** *"And as Moses lifted up the serpent in the wilderness, even so must the Son of man be lifted up: That whosoever believeth in him should not perish, but have eternal life"*. **John 3:36** reads *"He that believeth on the Son hath everlasting life: and he that believeth not the Son shall not see life; but the wrath of God abideth on him"*. **1 John 5:11-12** says *"And this is the record, that God hath given to us eternal life, and this life is in his Son. He that hath the Son hath life; and he that hath not the Son of God hath not life"*. We have a choice to accept the payment Christ made for us or reject it and try to pay for ourselves. Throughout the Bible, there is no single verse that promises eternal life to people who obey the law. Every time eternal or everlasting life is promised, it goes with full faith in the finished work of Jesus Christ. It is by changing our mind completely about our ability to save ourselves and accepting the full payment Jesus Christ made for us ALONE by faith that we receive eternal life from God. This is why Christians are called BELIEVERS – People who believe in Jesus Christ as their Saviour. This is why our works of righteousness cannot save us from hell or buy us eternal life in Heaven.

Some people believe that we need to accept the atonement made by Christ and also add our own works. We read in **Romans 11:6** that Salvation cannot come by both grace and works *"And if by grace, then is it no more of works: otherwise grace is no more grace. But if it be of works, then is it no more grace: otherwise work is no more work"*. It is arrogance to think that I can add something to what Jesus Christ did for us to pay for our sins. It is either we accept that He paid the price fully or we pay for our sins ourselves in hell. Jesus Christ did not perform a partial transaction on the cross. His suffering and death were more than enough to pay for just a part of our sins. He paid fully for the sins of the whole world, past, present and future. Before His death, John the Baptist described Him as *"…the Lamb of God, which taketh away the sin of the world"*(**John 1:29**). O what a Saviour!

Because salvation is free, it cannot be lost. We cannot lose our salvation once we are saved for several reasons. First, when we believe, we receive the Holy Spirit immediately and our salvation is sealed by the Holy Spirit according to **Ephesians 1:13** *"In whom ye also trusted, after that ye heard the word of truth, the gospel of your salvation: in whom also after that ye believed, ye were sealed with that holy Spirit of promise,"*. Second, we are adopted into the family of God as sons. We read in **John 1:12** *"But as many as received him, to them gave he power to become the sons of God, even to them that believe on his name:"*. **Galatians 3:26** says *"For ye are all the children of God by faith in Christ Jesus"*. Third, God has promised that He will never in any case disown His children in **John 6:37** *"All that the Father giveth me shall come to me; and him that cometh to me I will in no wise cast out"*. Fourth, God has promised that nothing can take us out of His hands once we become believers according to **John 10:27-29** *"My sheep hear my voice, and I know them, and they follow me: And I give unto them eternal life; and they shall never perish, neither shall any man pluck them out of my hand. My Father, which gave them me, is greater* *than all; and no man is able to pluck them out of my Father's hand"*. Fifth, the believer has passed from death unto life according to **John 5:24** *"Verily, verily, I say unto you, He that heareth my word, and believeth on him that sent me, hath everlasting life, and shall not come into condemnation; but is passed from death unto life"*. Finally, our salvation is kept by God. We read in **1 Peter 1:3-5** *"Blessed be the God and Father of our Lord Jesus Christ, which according to his abundant mercy hath begotten us again unto a lively hope by the resurrection of Jesus Christ from the dead, To an inheritance incorruptible, and undefiled, and that fadeth not away, reserved in heaven for you, **Who are kept by the power of God through faith unto salvation ready to be revealed in the last time"***. Wherever God promised eternal life in the scriptures, the promise is immediate for everyone who believes the right thing about Jesus Christ. It is not something the believer earns in the future as some people wrongly believe. You cannot lose something that is "eternal", giving to you free at the account of Christ, sealed by the Holy Spirit who comes to live in you immediately and kept by God until the end of time. This is why the Gospel is called "GOOD

NEWS". Salvation by grace through the blood of Christ is the only Gospel taught in the whole Bible and consistent with the whole scripture. This is also the only Gospel preached in the old times by the early believers before the current false teachings of salvation by works found its way into the Church. Listen to the old hymns and it runs through almost every one of them. It is the truth. It is this assurance or eternal security that moved the Apostles and other devout men and women of old to give their lives willingly to be killed or martyred in defence of the Gospel. The early missionaries travelled to dangerous places with the Gospel and joyfully paid with their lives because of this assurance. No man or woman will die for something he is not sure of and cannot be sure of. That is why **1 John 5:13** says we can know that we have eternal life.

Works after Salvation

In **John 14:15** Christ said *"If ye love me, keep my commandments"*. He didn't say if we want to go to Heaven, we should keep His commandments. Heaven is not for sale. He said if we love Him, we should keep

His commandments. We demonstrate our love to God by keeping His commandments. What should motivate us to love God? The answer is in **1 John 4:19** *"We love him, because he first loved us"*. How did He show His love to us first? The Bible says *"But God commendeth his love toward us, in that, while we were yet sinners, Christ died for us"* (**Romans 5:8**). When we were still sinners, God demonstrated His love towards us first by sending His only begotten Son, Jesus Christ, to die for our sins. By believing in Him, we receive eternal life.

We owed a debt we could not pay and He paid a debt He did not owe. This should motivate us to love God. The believer keeps the law because he loves God. If we were keeping the law to pay for our sins or earn eternal life, we can't show any love to God by doing so, because we are doing it to pay for eternal life. Unconditional love is a free gift. People who believe in the false gospel of salvation by works live in fear and keep the law out of fear. Those who believe in the true Gospel of salvation through faith in the blood of Jesus Christ alone, keeps the law out of love for God and they live in complete peace with God.

When the LORD was asked about the greatest commandment in the Bible, He said "...*Thou shalt love the Lord thy God with all thy heart, and with all thy soul, and with all thy mind*" (**Matthew 22:37**). Our first obligation as believers is to love God with everything in us. That is only possible for those who understand just how much they are indebted to the LORD for their salvation. We owe God so much that no amount of work we do for Him in our entire lifetime will be enough to pay Him back for giving us His only begotten Son to die for our sins. This should keep us loving Him for the rest of our lives.

The LORD said the second greatest commandment is "...*Thou shalt love thy neighbour as thyself*" (**Matthew 22:39**). How do we love our neighbour as ourselves? What is the greatest gift we can give to people to show them that we love them just like we love ourselves? It is salvation. A man's greatest need is the forgiveness of his sins. All men are searching for ways to find eternal rest after death. The best way we can demonstrate our love for people is to give them the true Gospel of Jesus Christ. Therefore, in **Matthew 28:19-20**, we are commanded *"Go ye therefore, and teach all nations, baptizing them in the name of the Father, and of the Son, and of the Holy Ghost: Teaching them to observe all things whatsoever I have commanded you: and, lo, I am with you alway, even unto the end of the world. Amen"*. We are commanded to take the Gospel to all nations and every individual. Carrying out this commandment must also be motivated by our love for God and the unsaved people, fulfilling the two greatest commandments. The LORD said, every other commandment in the Bible fits into these two commandments. Works of righteousness gives us the moral authority required to preach the Gospel effectively. This is the reason why we must continue in good works after salvation (**Titus 3:8**). It is not to keep us saved but give us a good relationship with God and opportunities to be used by Him to reach out to others who need the Gospel.

Sin after Salvation

What happens if the believer refuses to keep the commandments of God after salvation? First, he will lose his fellowship with God, not his salvation. When

King David sinned against God, he didn't lose his salvation, he lost fellowship with God and that is why he asked God in **Psalm 51:12** "*Restore unto me **the joy of thy salvation; and uphold me with thy free spirit**". He didn't ask God to restore his salvation but the joy of His (God's) salvation which comes from his fellowship with God. The salvation is not his, he didn't earn it. It is God's salvation and he couldn't lose what he didn't earn. I have children at home and they sometimes disobey me. When that happens, our relationship may be impaired but they don't cease to be my children. If they regret their behaviour and ask for forgiveness, I will forgive and punish them for their disobedience. That will restore our fellowship, not their position as my children because that will never be affected by their obedience or disobedience. They didn't earn their position as my children and they can't keep it by trying to be good children. They should be obedient children because they love me.

Second, when a believer sin, he will be punished severely here on earth by God (**Hebrews 12: 6-11**). God chastens His children. King David was punished severely after sinning against God but we know that he is in Heaven today (**Romans 4**). Third, if the believer continues in sin after several warnings, he can actually be killed by God and taken to Heaven to be with the LORD (**1 John 5:16**). In **1 Corinthians 5**, there was a believer in the Church at Corinth who slept with his father's wife. That is a humongous sin in the sight of God and men, isn't it? Paul, the Apostle wrote to them and in **verse 5** he asked the Church *"To deliver such an one unto Satan for the destruction of the flesh, that the spirit may be saved in the day of the Lord Jesus."* The Church was to break fellowship with that believer but Paul made it clear that, although from that moment, Satan could have access to his body to destroy it, but his soul will be saved. Fourth, the believer who refuses to walk according to the will of God shall not earn any rewards at the judgement seat of Christ. There are two judgements in the Bible; the judgement seat of Christ, which is reserved for believers only (**2 Corinthians 5:10, Romans 14:10**) and the great white throne judgement where unbelievers will be judged (**Revelations 20:11-15**). At the judgement seat of Christ, believers shall be rewarded for the works they did for God. We read in **1 Corinthians 3:15** that *"If any man's work shall be burned, he shall suffer loss: but he himself shall be saved; yet so as by fire"*. Believers who lived carnally will not earn any rewards from God but their souls will be saved. Again, if our works count for salvation, why should we be rewarded for our good works at the Judgement seat of Christ? The man who described himself as the Chief of sinners, the Apostle Paul said he was waiting for his crown in Heaven (**2 Timothy 4:6-8**). Therefore, Salvation through faith in Christ Jesus does not give any license to sin freely. God always punishes sin, the difference is when and where we will be punished. The believer is punished fully on earth in love as a father chastens his child, the unbeliever is punished partly on earth and fully in hell as full payment for his sin.

The Workmanship of God

We read in **Ephesians 2:10** that *"For we are his workmanship, created in Christ Jesus unto good works, which God hath before ordained that we should walk in them"*. We become the workmanship of God after salvation. That is why God doesn't take us to Heaven immediately after salvation. There are many unsaved people in the world who are dying and going to hell. God is not happy when a person dies and goes to hell (**Ezekiel 18:23, 2 Peter 3:9**). Hell was created for Satan, not man.

The LORD has chosen to use believers as the main medium to reach out to the world. The believer is required to keep a strong testimony by walking according to the laws and commandments of God. This will make his life exceptional and peculiar in his neighbourhood and point people to God. We read in **1 Peter 2:12** *"Having your conversation honest among the Gentiles: that, whereas they speak against you as evildoers, they may by your good works, which they shall behold, glorify God in the day of visitation"*. The believer is then required to preach the Gospel. With the Holy Spirit and the Word of God, every believer is equipped to be used by the LORD for the rest of his life until God calls him home. But God does not use all believers for the same works. We read in **2 Timothy 2:20-21** *"But in a great house there are not only vessels of gold and of silver, but also* *of wood and of earth; and some to honour, and some to dishonour. If a man therefore purge himself from these, he shall be a vessel unto honour, sanctified, and meet for the master's use, and prepared unto every good work*". If we love God and obey Him fully and walk in His will, we build a good testimony that He can use for His purpose. We become like the vessels of gold. On the other hand, if we walk waywardly before God, we lose that testimony required to be used by God for great works. To have power with God to do great works for Him, we must walk in His perfect will. We will never be perfect people while on earth but we must desire to do His will and the Holy Spirit will work in us to create this desire.

God uses Evangelists to plant Churches. He ordains Pastors and Deacons to oversee the spiritual and physical needs of the Church, respectively. He uses obedient parents to raise children for Him. Similarly, He uses career workers and businessmen to preach the Gospel to many people in the workplace and fund the Great Commission. If you are not a Pastor or Deacon, you can still be used by God fully in your secular job if you choose to obey Him wholly and avail yourself as a vessel to honour. Ministry or working in the Church is not the most important work of the believer. Our utmost responsibility is to obey God wherever we are and in whatever we do. We are to find His will by studying the Word of God and commit ourselves to do it. God can use us in any position He has placed us if we obey Him fully.

We know that Evangelist, Pastors and Deacons have been called to serve the LORD. What many believers don't know is that we have been called by God to serve Him fully wherever He chooses to place us and this include our workplaces. This is the reason why many believers are unproductive in the workplace. It is also the major reason why many believers are unable to propagate the Gospel in their workplaces. This book is written, first of all, to help the believer understand that he has been called by God to serve Him fully wherever he is placed, including his workplace. The doctrine presented in the book will help a willing believer to build a strong testimony with his work in his workplace that the LORD can use to reach out to the unsaved.

Summary

We are all sinners and the wages of sin is death. We cannot pay for our sins with good works because the only acceptable payment for our sins is blood. Jesus Christ died and shed His blood to pay fully for all our sins. Those who accept this payment shall be saved. The ten commandments do not play any role in salvation. However, before salvation, the Holy Spirit uses the Law to convict us of sin and lead us to repentance. After salvation, we keep the law to show our love towards God. We are His workmanship called to love the LORD and work for Him. The believer who works a full-time or part-time job can serve the LORD fully in the workplace. This book explains how we can honour God with our work after salvation.

REASONS TO WORK

"But Jesus answered them, My Father worketh hitherto, and I work." **John 5:17**

Why should we work? You might think this is a trivial question but the answer you provide to this simple question will determine your motivation to work, how you apply yourself to your work and the output of your work. There are many reasons why people work. Some work to meet their daily needs, raise money, accumulate wealth, power and fame. Others work for the love of the job, to keep family tradition or to win the approval of society. There are several reasons why people work. As believers, why should we work?

The standard set by God for the believer in the workplace is very high. To live up to that standard, our motivation must be right and align fully with the will of God. To serve God with our work, our hearts must be right with God. The main reason why believers are discouraged in the workplace is because their motivation is not right. If we have the right motivation, we will love our work and put in our best effort to honour God with our work. Let us turn to the Bible for answers to this all-important question: why must we work?

1. ***To follow God's example:*** God the Father worked for six days and on the seventh day He rested from all His work according to **Genesis 2:2** *"And on the seventh day God ended his work which he had made; and he rested on the seventh day from all his work which he had made"*. Our LORD, Jesus Christ, while on earth, also worked to follow the example of His Father as we read in **John 5:17** *"But Jesus answered them, My Father worketh hitherto, and I work"*. As children of God, we are commanded to be followers of God in **Ephesians 5:1** *"Be ye therefore followers of God, as dear children;"*. If our LORD worked to follow the example of God the Father, we must also work to follow Their example.

2. *To keep God's commandments*: In **John 14:15**, our LORD Jesus Christ charged us *"If ye love me, keep my commandments"*. We are commanded to work in **2 Thessalonians 3:11-12** *"For we hear that there are some which walk among you disorderly, working not at all, but are busybodies. Now them that are such we **command** and **exhort** by our Lord Jesus Christ, that with quietness they work, and eat their own bread"*. This commandment is repeated in **1 Thessalonians 4:11-12** *"And that ye study to be quiet, and to do your own business, and to work with your own hands, as we **commanded** you; That ye may walk honestly toward them that are without, and that ye may have lack of nothing"*. Most believers do not know that we are commanded to work. No matter how rich we are, we are still commanded to work. We are commanded to work with our hands, things that are good in the sight of God according to **Ephesians 4:28** *"Let him that stole steal no more: but rather let him labour, **working with his hands***

the thing which is good, *that he may have to give to him that needeth".*

3. *To Witness*: For believers, the workplace is a mission field. God provides us jobs in specific workplaces to share our testimony and preach the Gospel. We are commanded in **Matthew 5:16** *"Let your light so shine before men, **that they may see your good works, and glorify your Father which is in** heaven".* Our output at work should stand out for everyone to see. As the light of the world, we ought to shine wherever the LORD chooses to place us. It is our attitude at work that should draw the unsaved to God. Secondly, we are commanded to bear fruit in **John 15:16** *"Ye have not chosen me, but I have chosen you, and ordained you, that ye should go and bring forth fruit, and that your fruit should remain:...".* It is not enough to build a strong testimony at work. We must use our testimony to propel the Gospel in our workplaces.

4. *To provide for ourselves and other people*: Perhaps, provision is the most obvious reason why many people work. Naturally, our basic needs of food, clothing and shelter compel us to work (**Proverbs 16:26**). The Apostle Paul commanded the Church in Thessalonica that those who do not work should not eat in **2 Thessalonians 3:10** "*For even when we were with you, this we commanded you, that if any would not work, neither should he eat*". We work to at least provide our basic needs. In **1 Timothy 5:8** we read that "*But if any provide not for his own, and specially for those of his own house, he hath denied the faith, and is worse than an infidel*". We are also encouraged to work so that we can have enough to give to the needy (**Ephesians 4:28**). In reality, God is our provider (**Matthew 6:31-34, Philippians 4:19**). The LORD is able to provide more or less than what our actual labour deserves. For example, the value of your income decreases significantly if part of the money is used to pay unexpected expenses such as medical bills. On the other

hand, if God gives you the grace to spend the money without any unforeseen challenges, its value increases (**Ecclesiastes 5:19**). As long as we obey the LORD and work according to His will, He has promised to always supply our needs.

5. *To earn rewards*: As we follow in God's example and work according to His will, He has promised to provide our physical needs and eventually reward our good works according to **Job 34:11** *"For the work of a man shall he render unto him, and cause every man to find according to his ways"*. At the judgment seat of Christ, the LORD shall reward us according to our works as promised in **Matthew 16:27** *"For the Son of man shall come in the glory of his Father with his angels; and then he shall reward every man according to his works"* and **1 Corinthians 3:8** *"Now he that planteth and he that watereth are one: and every man shall receive his own reward according to his own labour"*. We are also promised in **Revelation 22:12** *"And, behold, I come quickly; and my reward is with me, to give every man according as his work shall be."*

Therefore, let us labour cheerfully for our LORD because He is the rewarder of those who diligently seek Him.

How to Choose a Good Job

If we want to honour God with our work, we must allow the LORD to direct our career. God has a special mission field for every believer. He might not necessarily lead us into a job that pays a huge salary and sometimes He won't provide a very attractive working environment. But as a child of God, the best place to be is in the will of God. Every believer who wants to serve the LORD with his work should first of all make sure that His choice of work is within the will of God because God does not work outside His will. What should guide the believer in choosing a job?

1. *We are called unto good works*: We read in **Ephesians 2:10** *"For we are his workmanship, created in Christ Jesus unto good works, which God hath before ordained that we should walk in them."* A believer should choose a job that has a positive impact on society. For example, working in a

brewery does not impact society positively. Working for a company that short-changes people is not a good job. As we are called unto good works, the output of our work must be good in the sight of God (**Ephesians 4:28**). Ask yourself this question: "would the LORD himself work in that position or company if He was offered the job?"

2. *We are to abstain from all appearance of evil*: We are commanded in **1 Thessalonians 5:22** *"Abstain from all appearance of evil"*. Don't accept a job in a position where you are frequently surrounded by evil practices and constantly tempted to sin against the LORD. Evil communication corrupt good manners (**1 Corinthians 15:33**). A job, where you are surrounded by colleagues who constantly lie, curse and take bribes could influence your character in the long term. Working for a betting company puts you in a tempting environment where you could be lured into gambling. Abstain from such kinds of jobs as much as possible.

3. *We are not called to help God*: Some believers have tried to justify working in a brewery because the salary is so good that they are convinced their tithes and offerings can make a positive impact on the Church. That is a clear case of man trying to help God. When Uzzah tried to help God, he got himself killed instantly (**1 Samuel 6:7**). Can a man help God? The God we serve is a living God. He doesn't need the help of man. He requires obedience rather than sacrifice as we read in **1 Samuel 15:22** *"And Samuel said, Hath the LORD as great delight in burnt offerings and sacrifices, as in obeying the voice of the LORD? Behold, **to obey is better than sacrifice**, and to hearken than the fat of rams"*. Our God does not require the help of man or any uncircumcised offering to build His Church. He said, *"I will build my Church…"* (**Matthew 16:18**). Never take a sinful job to help God because it is not in the place of man to help the LORD. Be guided by His will and walk humbly before Him in

obedience. That is all He require from His children (**Micah 6:8**).

4. *Let God provide the job*: God will supply all our need including a job as we read in **Philippians 4:19** *"But my God shall supply all your need according to his riches in glory by Christ Jesus."* However, the LORD only has a prepared place for a prepared person. Be not deceived, the LORD will not give you a job in a position where you are not qualified to serve. You may not be the most qualified person for the job but at least you need to meet the minimum entry qualifications for God to offer you the job because He is placing you there so that He can use the testimony of your work to win souls. He will not place us where we would bring shame and disrepute to His name. If you are not qualified to work in the position, don't use any dubious means outside the will of God to land the job. If you go outside the will of God to get a job, you may have to stay outside the will of God to keep it. Paying bribes, offering sex and

scheming your way into a job probably because of money or prestige is not within the will of God. The LORD will not bless such a job and definitely, He won't use you there.

5. *Never choose a job because of the money*: The Bible warns us in **Proverbs 23:4** *"Labour not to be rich: cease from thine own wisdom."* As children of God, we shouldn't choose a job because we THINK it will make us rich. Our provision comes from God and He has promised to provide all our needs as long as we stay within His will. It is not the person who earns a big salary that gets ahead, it is the blessings of the LORD that maketh rich according to **Proverbs 10:22** *"The blessing of the LORD, it maketh rich, and he addeth no sorrow with it"*. True riches with no sorrow come only from the LORD. Therefore, the wise man wrote in **Proverbs 15:16** *"Better is little with the fear of the LORD than great treasure and trouble therewith"*. The LORD is able to bless us regardless of our jobs as long as we labour according to His will and for His purpose.

Accept any job that the LORD provides and He will bless the work of your hands.

6. *Choose the job that has a high soul-winning potential*: In the sight of God, a single soul is worth more than the whole world and all its resources put together as implied in **Mark 8:36** *"For what shall it profit a man, if he shall gain the whole world, and lose his own soul?"*. God measures our success in terms of souls won and the potential to win souls. We must have a soul-winning mindset in everything we do. Always ask "what is in it for God?". In the sight of God, a cobbler who honours God with his work and wins souls through his job is more successful than a neurosurgeon who is not a believer even if he is the best. Choose a job that offers the best chance to serve God on and off the job. A job that requires you to work for seven days a week is not a good job regardless of the salary because it prevents you from attending Church services, especially on Sundays. A job that does not give you enough time with your family is also not a

good job because you need that contact time to win your family for the LORD. A good job should offer the best opportunity to share your testimony, give you enough time daily to train your children in the LORD, provide time to go soul-winning and attend Church meetings regularly.

Slothfulness

Slothfulness or laziness is a sin that destroys the testimony of a believer. Since we are commanded to work, we disobey God when we refuse to work. Also, as we represent the LORD in our workplaces, we bring shame and disrepute to His name when we work below the standards required of us. The biggest challenge of the Christian worker today is not idleness but mediocrity. We are working far below the standards required by the LORD. Laziness is not the refusal to work but working just enough to get paid.

Characteristics of slothful people

The following are some of the characteristics of slothful people:

1. *They are not diligent*: A major attribute of lazy people is that they are not careful and persistent in the execution of their duties. They rush through their work. They simply put in the minimum effort required to satisfy the task at hand as we read in **Proverbs 12:24** *"The slothful man roasteth not that which he took in hunting: but the substance of a diligent man is precious"*. Slothful workers do their best but diligent workers do the best. Slothful workers work to get paid whilst diligent people work to honour God.

2. *They always find excuses*: slothful people always come up with reasons to explain their failure. Some use fear as an excuse according to **Proverbs 22:13** *"The slothful man saith, There is a lion without, I shall be slain in the streets."* Others blame the weather for their failure to work well as we read in **Proverbs 20:4** *"The sluggard will not plow by reason of the cold; therefore shall he beg in*

harvest, and have nothing". People who often complain or find excuses are lazy. Diligent people accept responsibility and always find a way to get things done even under unfavourable conditions.

3. *They are not wise*: We read in **Proverbs 6:6** "*Go to the ant, thou sluggard; consider her ways, and be wise.*". Slothful people often try to outsmart employers by putting in minimum effort for maximum rewards as written in **Proverbs 26:16** "*The sluggard is wiser in his own conceit than seven men that can render a reason*". After scheming for a while, their image is tarnished and they are the first to be laid off in times of crisis. Many artisans have lost potential clients because of gross insolence displayed in executing past tasks.

4. *They are wasteful*: slothful people are also great wasters according to **Proverbs 18:9** "*He also that is slothful in his work is brother to him that is a great waster*". Lazy people often waste money on unnecessary expenditure. They lack the ability to manage time and resources effectively. They love

pleasure and spend money on anything that pleases them as they don't really earn the money with appropriate investment of labour. They often waste time on simple tasks and intentionally delay jobs in attempt to earn more from daily wages. They also waste resources in their work.

5. *They love sleep*: Slothful people love sleep according to **Proverbs 19:15** *"Slothfulness casteth into a deep sleep; and an idle soul shall suffer hunger."* They don't rise early out of sleep and are often late for work as written in **Proverbs 6:9** *"How long wilt thou sleep, O sluggard? when wilt thou arise out of thy sleep?"* Although the slothful spend a lot of time on bed, they don't really enjoy their sleep according to **Proverbs 26:14** *"As the door turneth upon his hinges, so doth the slothful upon his bed"*. On the other hand, the Bible says in **Ecclesiastes 5:12** *"The sleep of a labouring man is sweet, whether he eat little or much..."*. Lazy people spend more hours of their day in bed. Diligent people wake up early because they crave

for work. Early to sleep and early to rise make a man wise, healthy and wealthy.

6. *They are wicked*: slothfulness in itself is wickedness in the sight of God. By being slothful, we deny God the opportunity to use us in our workplaces. In addition, slothful people often want great rewards for their shoddy work. We read in **Matthew 25:26** *"His lord answered and said unto him, **Thou wicked and slothful servant,** thou knewest that I reap where I sowed not, and gather where I have not strawed."* Slothful people are cheats and often master the subtle art of short-changing people for a living.

The consequences of slothfulness

Like every wicked sin in the Bible, slothfulness has grave consequences including the following:

1. *Poverty and hunger*: Poverty is the main consequence of slothfulness as written in **Proverbs 13:4** *"The soul of the sluggard desireth, and hath nothing: but the soul of the diligent shall be made fat"* and **Proverbs 20:4** *"The sluggard will*

not plow by reason of the cold; therefore shall he beg in harvest, and have nothing". Lazy people also suffer hunger as we read in **Proverbs 19:15** *"Slothfulness casteth into a deep sleep; and an idle soul shall suffer hunger"*. Because the slothful are often idle, they tend to get hungry more often. Lazy people eat a lot. The diligent on the other hand prove themselves trustworthy, earn higher responsibility and reap the rewards of their labour.

2. *Dependency*: We read in **Proverbs 12:24** *"The hand of the diligent shall bear rule: but the slothful shall be under tribute"*. The slothful are often ruled by the diligent. In terms of position, the diligent rise faster in the workplace and rule over the slothful. In finances, the diligent earn much higher than the slothful. Since the slothful is also a great waster, he borrows from the diligent to meet his extravagant lifestyle. We read in the Bible that the borrower is servant to the lender (**Proverbs 22:7**).

3. *Suffering*: The life of the slothful is characterised by suffering as written in **Proverbs 15:19** *"The way of the slothful man is as an hedge of thorns: but the way of the righteous is made plain"*. The slothful lives a confused life with no sense of direction and certainty. By trying to find an easy way of life, they end up paying dearly for lack of wisdom. Their ways are crooked and most of the time they survive through scheming. They spend a lot of time on bed but hardly get good sleep. They have no assurance of success. The diligent on the other hand live a plain lifestyle, with well-defined goals and a sense of purpose and direction.

4. *Unfulfilled desires*: We read in **Proverbs 21:25** *"The desire of the slothful killeth him; for his hands refuse to labour"*. Slothful people have high desires and ambitions that are never fulfilled because they refuse to work towards them. With high ambitions and desires and not prepared to work, most slothful people often resort to crime and fraud to meet their desires. The LORD has

promised to give us the desires of our hearts if we live according to His will which includes working with our hands to present a strong testimony in our workplaces for Him.

Summary

As believers, we work to honour the LORD. Our testimony in the workplace is one of the most powerful tools the LORD uses to propel the Gospel. The LORD will supply all our needs including the need for a job. In searching for jobs, let us be careful not to put our personal ambitions above the will of God. Slothfulness is a sin that destroys our testimony and reduces our ability to win souls in the workplace. Let us labour diligently to honour the LORD in our workplaces and present ourselves, worthy vessels meet for the Master's use.

ATTITUDE AT WORK

"Whatsoever thy hand findeth to do, do it with thy might; for there is no work, nor device, nor knowledge, nor wisdom, in the grave, whither thou goest." **Ecclesiastes 9:10**

Our attitude at work, determines to a large extent, how the LORD will use us in the workplace. If we labour diligently, the LORD will bless the work of our hands and create more opportunities for soul-winning. If our attitude towards work falls below the standards required by God, we won't find fulfilment in our work. Therefore, it is imperative to know the right attitude the LORD require of us in our workplaces.

Who do we work for?

Paul, the Apostle asked in **Galatians 1:10** *"For do I now persuade men, or God? or do I seek to please men? for if I yet pleased men, I should not be the servant of Christ."* In practice, we work for the employer, but in principle, we work for God. As children of God, the LORD provides the job, making us accountable to Him. Our first and most important attitude at work should be people who work for God. This should be our mindset in everything we do in our workplaces. We don't work to please men or earn the approval of people. Our attitude at work should not change in the presence or absence of supervisors. We are the workmanship of God. The work environment and remuneration should not in any way influence our sense of diligence and motivation at work. We should be known as people who work for God. Every workplace is a mission field where we are called and sent to work for the LORD.

As believers in the workplace, if we are being underpaid, the proper thing to do is to take it to the LORD in prayer and seek His direction. If we work for God, our reward should come from Him. All our dissatisfaction at work should be channelled to Him in prayer. The LORD, who is a rewarder of those who diligently seek Him is more than faithful to resolve every challenge in our work. Actually, if we develop the attitude of people who work for God, we may never need to strive for better working conditions. Using unlawful means to push for higher rewards is out of the will of God and this could tarnish our testimony at work.

Similarly, every task assigned to us at work is directed by God. We shouldn't complain or murmur when we are assigned a more challenging task. God allows tasks to be assigned to us to build a character in us or achieve a divine objective (**Philippians 2:14-15**). If we develop this mindset properly, nothing can discourage us at work. There is no better motivation to achieve more at work than waking up every morning with the conviction that we are employees of Jesus Christ in the workplace.

Our reputation at work

Believers should be known as diligent or hard workers. Our reputation at work should be that of diligent people who strive for excellence in everything they do, because that is the character of our God. All the works of God are perfect. We, being His followers, ought to demonstrate His character of excellence in every task assigned to us. People should see the character of God in the way we work and His excellence in the work of our hands. We are commanded in **Ecclesiastes 9:10** "*Whatsoever thy hand findeth to do, do it with thy might; for there is no work, nor device, nor knowledge, nor wisdom, in the grave, whither thou goest*". Our reputation at work should be so strong and clear that it will encourage employers to hire more believers. In an ideal world, believers should be hired without an interview. Such should be our testimony at work. We should be known as diligent, loyal, dependable and skilled workers who give everything in whatever task we are assigned at work. Whatsoever our hands find to do – that is any task assigned to us, whether it pays well or not, we must work with all our might. Which employer would not want to hire a worker with such reputation?

Communication at work

Communication is a slippery area that can destroy the testimony of the believer in the workplace. We learn that *"Not that which goeth into the mouth defileth a man; but that which cometh out of the mouth, this defileth a man."* (**Matthew 15:11**). If we learn to communicate properly, it will enhance our relationship with the LORD and strengthen our testimony at work. What comes out of our mouths purifies or defiles us. Thus, it is always important to allow the LORD to speak through us at work.

First, we should put off all filthy communication at work as commanded in **Colossians 3:8** *"But now ye also put off all these; anger, wrath, malice, blasphemy, **filthy communication out of your mouth**"*. What we say at work should match our actions. We should be known as people who live our word. We should not be known as loose talkers who speak before they think about what they have said. As we read in **1 Corinthians 15:33** *"Be not deceived: evil communications corrupt good manners"*. If we profess to be believers and our words indicate otherwise, it demonstrates confusion. Filthy communication often goes with anger and wrath. We must learn to control ourselves and speak less when we are angry. Anger, in itself, is not a sin but it should not lead us to sin as commanded in **Ephesians 4:26** *"Be ye angry, and sin not: let not the sun go down upon your wrath:"*. We should be filled with the Holy Spirit always and learn to keep silent when we are angry.

Second, the believer should have the reputation of truthfulness at work as we are commanded in **Colossians 3:9** *"Lie not one to another, seeing that ye have put off the old man with his deeds"*. We must tell the truth without fear in every situation. In addition, our word should demonstrate power. Let us learn to keep our word so that people can trust what we say. Let us strive to avoid making empty or vain promises at work. Every unkept promise cast a dent on our testimony. In a nutshell *"...let your communication be, Yea, yea; Nay, nay: for whatsoever is more than these cometh of evil"* (**Matthew 5:37**).

Third, we must avoid profane language in all our communication as commanded in **2 Timothy 2:16** *"But shun profane and vain babblings: for they will increase unto more ungodliness"*. Profanity defiles the believer and increases ungodliness. We lose power to share the Gospel with people we have engaged in profane conversations. Unbelievers hold believers to higher standards than the believer may even know. When trust is broken, it discourages unbelievers and serves as a stumbling block to them coming to a saving knowledge of the LORD. The believer should not engage in profane and filthy jokes, also called jesting. Let us demonstrate purity in all our communication.

Finally, all our communication must demonstrate empathy and the grace of God according to **Ephesians 4:29** *"Let no corrupt communication proceed out of your mouth, but that which is good to the use of edifying, that it may minister grace unto the hearers"*. We should be people who carry positive energy at work. We should encourage those who are cast down, strengthen the weak and motivate people at work. Believers should not be seen as gossipers and backbiters at work. Backbiting has been listed as one of the characters of reprobates in **Romans 1:30** *"Backbiters, haters of God, despiteful, proud, boasters, inventors of evil things, disobedient to parents,"*. Badmouthing people destroys our chances of reaching out to them and winning them over for the LORD. We should pray for our enemies and do good to those who hate us, perhaps the LORD might use us to convert them.

Our thoughts at work

We read in **Proverbs 23:7** *"For as he thinketh in his heart, so is he:"*. Our thoughts shape our lives. As children of God, what we think about is very important to the LORD. To present a strong testimony at work with our speech and actions, we must have the right thoughts. If our thoughts are continually evil, our speech and actions will not be any different as we read in **Proverbs 15:26** *"The thoughts of the wicked are an abomination to the LORD: but the words of the pure are pleasant words"*. God hates evil thoughts. Therefore, it is important to know what the LORD wants us to think about at work.

We are instructed in **Philippians 4:8** *"Finally, brethren, whatsoever things are true, whatsoever things are honest, whatsoever things are just, whatsoever things are pure, whatsoever things are lovely, whatsoever things are of good report; if there be any virtue, and if there be any praise, think on these things"*. This scripture summarizes everything the LORD wants us to think about as follows:

1. *We are to think about things that are true*: many false rumours circulate in the workplace. Rumours, gossip, false accusations, fake news, wrong impressions people may have about us and several false information pushed around at work. We should be

careful not to waste our thoughts on these things but rather think about things that are true. Our thoughts must not be influenced by worldly philosophies that are mostly false and merely human opinions.

2. *We should think about things that are honest*: we must think about things that are honest, free of deceit. Our thoughts should be truthful devoid of any intention to lie or deceive people. The object of our thoughts should be to reflect the character of God.

3. *We should think about things that are just*: we must be just in our thoughts because justice is the character of God. In our thoughts, we must treat people the same way we would treat ourselves. Let us learn to treat people equally in our thoughts.

4. *We should think about things that are pure*: filthy thoughts defile the believer. Lustful and impure thoughts corrupt our attitudes and increase our chances of defiling ourselves through sexual sins. Let us learn to think about things that are pure and edifying.

5. *We should think about things that are lovely*: everything we think about should be motivated by love. There is no room for wickedness in the

thoughts of a believer because the thoughts of the wicked is an abomination to the LORD. Let us learn to clean our thoughts of all evil and wickedness and fill them with lovely thoughts.

6. *We should think about things that are of good report*: we should always ask ourselves if our thoughts are acceptable before God and man. Would you be proud if people knew what you were thinking about right now? Let us think about things that will give a good account of us before God and our fellow men.

7. *We should think about things that have virtue and praise*: let us subject all our thoughts to the highest standards of God's word. Our thoughts should be praiseworthy.

We are admonished in **Proverbs 16:3** *"Commit thy works unto the LORD, and thy thoughts shall be established"*. If we work for the LORD and commit every work to Him, He will help us keep our thoughts in check. If we are always focused on serving God and pleasing Him in everything we do, it will be very difficult to have evil thoughts, as they will be clouded out with the thoughts of our master, Jesus Christ. We read in **Romans 12:2** *"And be not conformed to this world: but be ye transformed by the renewing of your mind, that ye may prove* *what is that good, and acceptable, and perfect, will of God"*. We can renew our minds by constantly meditating on the Word of God.

Your Relationship with Your Boss

We must learn to manage relationships at work if we are to be used by God. The most important relationship at work is your relationship with your immediate boss. The Bible teaches us about how to relate with our leaders and those in authority in **Romans 13:1-7** *"Let every soul be subject unto the higher powers. For there is no power but of God: the powers that be are ordained of God. Whosoever therefore resisteth the power, resisteth the ordinance of God: and they that resist shall receive to themselves damnation. For rulers are not a terror to good works, but to the evil. Wilt thou then not be afraid of the power? do that which is good, and thou shalt have praise of the same: For he is the minister of God to thee for good. But if thou do that which is evil, be afraid; for he beareth not the sword in vain: for he is the minister of God, a revenger to execute wrath upon him that doeth evil. Wherefore ye must needs be subject, not only for wrath, but also for conscience sake. For for this cause pay ye tribute also: for they are God's ministers, attending continually upon this very thing. Render therefore to all their dues: tribute to whom tribute* *is due; custom to whom custom; fear to whom fear; honour to whom honour"*. From this scripture, we learn that:

1. **People in authority are placed there by God:** *"For there is no power but of God: the powers that be are ordained of God"*.

2. **If we disobey our boss, we disobey God:** *"Whosoever therefore resisteth the power, resisteth the ordinance of God"*.

3. **The boss is not there for evil:** *"For rulers are not a terror to good works, but to the evil"*.

4. **If you work right, you will receive their praise:** *"do that which is good, and thou shalt have praise of the same"*.

5. **The boss is a minister of God to punish those who don't work right:** *"But if thou do that which is evil, be afraid; for he beareth not the sword in vain: for he is the minister of God, a revenger to execute wrath upon him that doeth evil"*.

6. **Submit to your boss for the sake of conscience:** *"Wherefore ye must needs be subject, not only for wrath, but also for conscience sake"*.

The chain of command is also very clear in **Romans 13:1-7**. As children of God, the LORD is our ultimate head in the workplace. Leaders or authority in the workplace are simply people he has positioned over us to pass down His instructions. Thus, as a believer at work, every instruction or task which is not against the Word of God is passed down from the LORD through the authority. If the instruction or task is against the Word of God, definitely it is not from the LORD and we must resist it politely. For example, if your boss instructs you to commit sexual sin or take a bribe, you must turn down the advances.

You might say "ah! this people don't know my wicked boss; how can I respect and honour such a boss who hates me so much?". The scripture doesn't say godly and caring bosses are placed in authority by God and that they are the only ministers of God in the workplace. It says all leaders in every workplace, and that includes your boss *"For there is no power but of God"*.

Before we delve into the nuts and bolts of this subject, there is a general principle of God every believer must know. The commandments of God don't have exceptions. Yet, all His commandments are motivated by love and there is no wickedness in Him (**Psalm 92:15**). The LORD knows all the challenges and consequences associated with choosing to obey His commandments. He only requires us to trust and obey Him. When we overlook the challenges and take the first step in obedience, He handles the challenges and consequences or gives grace to endure them in immense peace and joy. That is how our relationship with God works.

The LORD knows your boss very well, actually if you are a child of God, the LORD intentionally placed you under His authority to nurture a certain character in you or so that He can use you to convert your boss or fulfil His will in that environment. He knows all your challenges at work. If you obey Him and take the first step to work according to His Word, He will give you the grace to succeed and enjoy your work.

When you sign an employment contract or offer, you must give what you have promised on the contract; respect, fear, hard work, and honour. But how can we fulfil this scripture in the workplace? The following are a few guidelines.

First, we are commanded to always pray for our leaders: we read in **1 Timothy 2:1** *"I exhort therefore, that, first of all, supplications, prayers, intercessions, and giving of thanks, be made for all men; For kings, and for all that are in authority;*

that we may lead a quiet and peaceable life in all godliness and honesty". Note that the reason we have been asked to pray for people in authority is so that *"we may lead a quiet and peaceable life in all godliness and honesty"*. Even if we are not happy with the boss, at least we want to live a peaceable life in all godliness and honesty in our workplaces. The LORD says He will see to that if only we pray for those in authority. The commandment is simple; pray for your boss, nothing else is important. Your feelings about your boss should not be an excuse.

Second, we must not always expect to know why the boss wants us to carry out every task: we read in **John 15:15** *"Henceforth I call you not servants; **for the servant knoweth not what his lord doeth:** but I have called you friends; for all things that I have heard of my Father I have made known unto you"*. Sometimes leaders may explain things and seek our opinion before they take certain decisions. However, we must know that they don't owe us any explanations as to why they want us to perform certain tasks. As long as the duty does not conflict with the Word of God, ours is to work and make sure we are working within the will of God. We must strive to avoid Complains, murmurings and unnecessary excuses (**Philippians 2:14-16**).

Third, we must obey our leaders in all things: we read in **Colossians 3:22-25** *"Servants, obey in all things your masters according to the flesh; not with eyeservice, as menpleasers; but in singleness of heart, fearing God: And whatsoever ye do, do it heartily, as to the Lord, and not unto men; Knowing that of the Lord ye shall receive the reward of the inheritance: for ye serve the Lord Christ. But he that doeth wrong shall receive for the wrong which he hath done: and there is no respect of persons"*. We are to obey our masters in all things. However, this is limited to the contract of the job. If we are asked to perform duties outside our work contract, tasks that are not against the Word of God, we should obey, perhaps the LORD will use it to give us soul winning opportunities. However, we should never perform a task that is against the Word of God. For example, if your boss asks you to spend time with him in a drinking pub, you must politely refuse. We also read in **Titus 2:9-10** *"Exhort servants to be obedient unto their own masters, and to please them well in all things; not answering again; Not purloining, but shewing all good fidelity; that they may adorn the doctrine of God our Saviour in all things."* Obedience is only the first time. If we don't obey at the first instruction, we have disobeyed. As believers, we must obey our leaders without complaining, so that we may adorn the doctrine of God in our workplaces. We are also admonished to obey our leaders even if they are unbelievers, for the sake of our conscience as we read in **1 Peter 2:18-20** *"Servants, be subject to your masters with all fear; not only to the good and gentle, but also to the froward. For this is thankworthy, if a man for conscience toward God endure grief, suffering wrongfully. For what glory is it, if, when ye be buffeted for your faults, ye shall take it patiently? but if, when ye do well, and suffer for it, ye take it patiently, this is acceptable with God"*.

Fourth, we must not expect special rewards before carrying out our duties: we read in **Luke 17:7-10** *"But which of you, having a servant plowing or feeding cattle, will say unto him by and by, when he is come from the field, Go and sit down to meat? And will not rather say unto him, Make ready wherewith I may sup, and gird thyself, and serve me, till I have eaten and drunken; and afterward thou shalt eat and drink?* **Doth he thank that servant because he did the things that were commanded him? I trow not.** *So likewise ye, when ye shall have done all those things which are commanded you, say, We are unprofitable servants: we have done that which was our duty to do."* Many workers tend to expect extra praise of men or special monetary rewards for carrying out duties they have already been paid to do. This is wrong and doesn't attract the blessings of God. Because bad financial decisions have put many workers under pressure, they tend to see every task as an opportunity to earn extra income. We should see every extra task as an opportunity to start a conversation or share the Gospel.

Fifth, we must honour our leaders: we read in **1 Timothy 6:1-2** *"Let as many servants as are under the yoke count their own masters worthy of all honour, that the name of God and his doctrine be not blasphemed. And they that have believing masters, let them not despise them, because they are brethren; but rather do them service, because they are faithful and beloved, partakers of the benefit. These things teach and exhort"*. We must give our leaders all the esteem, dignity and respect for the sake of the name of God. We as servants of Christ are representatives of God, and our leaders must see that in how we deal with them. We must not give our leaders any reason to blaspheme the name of God. The same respect and honour should be extended to leaders who are believers. Remember, we must honour leaders because it is commanded by God, not because they deserve it. That means we must honour them always, regardless of their attitude towards us.

Being a Leader in the Workplace

Similarly, the Word of God makes provision for believers in positions of authority in the workplace. Leadership positions present a special opportunity to influence both the people working under us, our colleagues and other authority above us. If you are a leader, God requires you to be guided by the following doctrine:

Pray for your workers: We read in **1 Timothy 2:1** *"I exhort therefore, that, first of all, supplications, prayers, intercessions, and giving of thanks, be made for all men;"*. We know that we should be praying for our leaders. However, the LORD also requires us to pray for those who work under us. Constant prayer for our workers will help us establish a stronger relationship with them, and also be a reminder that God put us there to be a testimony to them. It is also easier to deal with a person whom you pray for on a regular basis. Praying for those who work under us will give us a peaceful working environment, stronger working relationships and open more doors for us to witness to them.

Respect the chain of command: We read in **Matthew 6:24** *"No man can serve two masters: for either he will hate the one, and love the other; or else he will hold to the one, and despise the other..."*. Always remember the chain of command as you rise through the ranks. Don't remove yourself from the chain. The people who work under you can only follow you as you follow your superiors. You cannot expect to be an effective leader if you are constantly conflicting with other leaders above you. Respect authority and be loyal to those who have rule over you to set an example for those who work under you.

Treat your workers equally and justly: We read in **Colossians 4:1** *"Masters, give unto your servants that which is just and equal; knowing that ye also have a Master in heaven"*. Don't show favouritism; deal with each person and situation justly. As we move up the ladder in our workplaces, we need to assume a higher role of representing Christ. Once you become a leader, you have the opportunity to represent Christ as a leader. Our LORD is the just and perfect judge. As we advance, many times, we are put into situations that we become judges. This requires us to judge justly as followers of Christ.

Serve the will of God: The LORD said in **John 5:30** *"I can of mine own self do nothing: as I hear, I judge: and my judgment is just; because I seek not mine own will, but the will of the Father which hath sent me."* Even our leadership roles need to reflect our devotion to Christ. Just as Christ leads perfectly and cares for His followers, we need to represent him in that way of being good leaders and taking care of those who work under us that we may become a picture of what it means to serve under Christ. The will of God should always be our primary objective.

Respect your workers: We read in **Ephesians 6:5-9** *"Servants, be obedient to them that are your masters according to the flesh, with fear and trembling, in singleness of your heart, as unto Christ; Not with eyeservice, as menpleasers; but as the servants of Christ, doing the will of God from the heart; With good will doing service, as to the Lord, and not to men: Knowing that whatsoever good thing any man doeth, the same shall he receive of the Lord, whether he be bond or free. **And, ye masters, do the same things unto them, forbearing threatening: knowing that your master also is in heaven; neither is there respect of persons with him"**.* Just as we are supposed to respect our masters, we must also respect those who work for us. We cannot treat our workers any different than we treat those who are placed over us. We are also commanded to avoid threatening or being cruel or unjust to those placed under us. That is not a good representation of Christ. The LORD doesn't only care about how we represent him but also how we treat those that we have been put in charge.

Be led by Christ: Apostle Paul said in **1 Corinthians 11:1** *"Be ye followers of me, even as I also am of Christ."* Paul summarizes the leadership role very simply. Lift up those who are around you and try to lead them in the right way. We cannot force people, but we can point people in the right way. A good leader will gather a team to follow him rather than force his team to obey him. There are situations that cause us to rebuke those who are under us but it should be done fairly and justly for the purpose of lifting them up.

Pay your workers on time: We read in **Deuteronomy 24:15** *"At his day thou shalt give him his hire, neither shall the sun go down upon it; for he is poor, and setteth his heart upon it: lest he cry against thee unto the LORD, and it be sin unto thee"*. **Leviticus 19:13** says *"Thou shalt not defraud thy neighbour, neither rob him: the wages of him that is hired shall not abide with thee all night until the morning"*. And **1 Timothy 5:18** reads *"For the scripture saith, Thou shalt not muzzle the ox that treadeth out the corn. And, The labourer is worthy of his reward"*. One of the strongest testimonies a believer in authority can keep is one who pays his workers on time and deals justly with them financially. Always pay workers on time and be truthful to them. People in the world hold their finances in high esteem and many appreciate leaders who honour their promises.

Witnessing at work

We read in **Matthew 5:16** "*Let your light so shine before men, that they may see your good works, and glorify your Father which is in heaven*". First and foremost, our testimony is in how we work. We cannot hope to effectively witness to our colleagues if we don't have a testimony of being good workers. The two cannot go into conflict with each other. Even if we don't find opportunities to preach the Gospel, our testimony should reflect it. Our attitude at work should preach what we believe and our output should prove that we serve a living God.

But in **2 Timothy 4:2** we also read "*Preach the word; be instant in season, out of season; reprove, rebuke, exhort with all longsuffering and doctrine.*" We should be men of the Bible. Most workplaces offer some times in which we can talk with our colleagues. What do you talk about during your free time? Does the Bible mean enough to you that your conversation is built around it all the time? People get reputations based on what they often talk about. We should use our free time to preach and share the Gospel with our colleagues or at least create an environment to discuss spiritual issues.

We also read in **I Peter 3:15** – *"But sanctify the Lord God in your hearts: and be ready always to given an answer to every man that asketh you a reason of the hope what is in you with meekness and fear: having a good conscience; that, whereas they speak evil of you, as of evildoers, they may be ashamed that falsely accuse your good conversation in Christ"*. Believers must stand out as peculiar people in the workplace. If we live a life, separated unto the LORD, it will bring up questions from people. We should always be ready to give answers for why we live the way we do whether a short answer, brief explanation, or an invite to get together so that we can talk freely without the fear of interruption. We need to be ready to give answers and preach the Gospel.

Summary

Attitude is very important. Our attitude in the workplace will determine the extent of our influence and how God will use us. The LORD has given us clear doctrine to guide our words, thoughts, actions and our deeds in the workplace. God also made provision in the Bible for both leaders and subordinates in the workplace. We cannot expect God to use us effectively until we learn to work within His Word. If we work according to His Word, He blesses us and gives us more opportunities to witness to those around us and win souls for Christ. We pray the LORD will help us to obey His commandments and labour lawfully for Him in our workplaces.

MEN WHO WORKED

"For whatsoever things were written aforetime were written for our learning, that we through patience and comfort of the scriptures might have hope." **Romans 15:4**

The Bible has the best mentors for believers. God has provided examples of devout men who were used to achieve great things for Him in their workplaces. By studying the life and works of these great men, we learn about their faith and devotion to God, the challenges they encountered in their workplaces and how the LORD dealt with them. Their testimonies should serve as examples for us as written in **1 Corinthians 10:11** *"Now all these things happened unto them for ensamples: and they are written for our admonition, upon whom the ends of the world are come"*. In this chapter, we examine the life of four devout men who worked for the LORD; Noah, Joseph, Daniel and Nehemiah. These men were selected out of the many to demonstrate how God works in different aspects of our workplaces. More importantly, their testimonies are timeless and we believe they are still very much applicable in today's dynamic and technology-driven workplace.

Noah - The Man who Obeyed God

There was a time when all the people on earth were completely wicked, rebellious and corrupt in the sight of God. The Bible describes the situation in **Genesis 6:5** *"And GOD saw that the wickedness of man was great in the earth, and that every imagination of the thoughts of his heart was only evil continually"*. In this absolutely wicked world, the Bible says in **Genesis 6:8** *"But Noah found grace in the eyes of the LORD"*. In **verse 9**, we learn more about the life of Noah *"These are the generations of Noah: Noah was a just man and perfect in his generations, and Noah walked with God"*. This scripture teaches us that the LORD will always preserve a remnant for Himself in every generation. There was never and there will never come a time when God will lack useful vessels for His work, regardless of the level of corruption in the world.

It was in the midst of this completely wicked world that God called Noah to work for Him in **Genesis 6:13-14** *"And God said unto Noah, The end of all flesh is come before me; for the earth is filled with violence through them; and, behold, I will destroy them with the earth. Make thee an ark of gopher wood; rooms shalt thou make in the ark, and shalt pitch it within and* *without with pitch*". The wickedness of man had reached its limit and God decided to destroy these wicked men together with the earth. Noah was assigned the task to make an ark that God was going to use to save the remnant of God during the flood. It was such an important task. Similarly, today, our world is dying to hell and God has assigned every believer the all-important task to preach the Gospel, win souls and save the world. What can we learn from Noah? In the call of Noah, we learn the following important lessons that we can readily apply in our workplaces.

First, leaders must strive to be concise and specific about every task and assignment. God always defines details of every task He assigns to His workers. He is not the author of confusion (**1 Corinthians 14:33**). In **Genesis 6:15-16**, the LORD specified details of Noah's assignment "*And this is the fashion which thou shalt make it of: The length of the ark shall be three hundred cubits, the breadth of it fifty cubits, and the height of it thirty cubits. A window shalt thou make to the ark, and in a cubit shalt thou finish it above; and the door of the ark shalt thou set in the side thereof; with lower, second, and third stories shalt thou make it*". Leaders in the workplace must always specify details of every task they assign to their workers. Instructions, guidelines, rules and regulations should be communicated clearly to workers. Those who work under us should always know exactly what we want from them and how they ought to conduct themselves. This minimizes confusion in the workplace. If you are a worker, when the details of a task are not specified, kindly ask for clarification. Before signing a work contract, always make sure the tasks, key performance indicators (KPIs), rules and regulations are clearly spelt out. Concise tasks and clear guidelines are key to effective execution.

Second, obedience means doing as commanded. In **Genesis 6:22** we read that Noah constructed the ark exactly as God had commanded *"Thus did Noah; according to all that God commanded him, so did he"*. In **Genesis 7:1-3**, God provided further instructions to Noah on who and what should be allowed into the ark before the flood. In **Genesis 7:5** we learn again that Noah did exactly what he was commanded *"And Noah did according unto all that the LORD commanded him"*. Noah didn't complain about the nature of the work, he didn't demand anything from the LORD, he did not ask God why things should be done the way he was commanded, he didn't suggest another way God could have solved the problem, he simply listened and did exactly what THE BOSS has commanded him to do. In **Colossians 3:22** we are commanded *"Servants, obey in all things your masters according to the flesh; not with eyeservice, as menpleasers; but in singleness of heart, fearing God:"*. Noah obeyed God and worked according to all His instructions. As the workmanship of God in the workplace, we ought to obey our masters in all things and work according to their instructions because that is the will of God.

How then do we become innovative if we don't question the rules and instructions? The law of obedience does not in any way discourage innovation. If you know another way to improve the work, first, execute the task exactly according to the instructions of your boss. Present the work to him and afterwards suggest how you think the work could be improved. Here is the secret. Because you obeyed and worked according to his initial instructions, your boss will not feel that you are looking for a way to reduce your workload or avoid the task. Since you executed the task according to instructions, he can trust your competence when you suggest a new way to improve the work. If you obey him first and give him what he wants, he will not feel threatened by your ideas, because, naturally we like to listen to people who obey and honour us. Finally, because you did as God has required of every worker, the LORD will give you favour in the sight of your boss when you suggest a new idea to him. Total obedience actually makes it easier to work creatively and inspire innovation in the workplace. It is the surest path to influence change in any workplace.

Third, we learn from the story of Noah that there is great reward for obedience. Noah obeyed God in all things and the LORD used him to save his family and raise a new earth. In every work, first of all, God requires absolute obedience according to **1 Samuel 15:22** *"And Samuel said, Hath the LORD as great delight in burnt offerings and sacrifices, as in obeying the voice of the LORD?* ***Behold, to obey is better than sacrifice, and to hearken than the fat of rams."*** Without obedience, even if we offer our lives to God, it will not please Him. God cannot use a proud, disobedient and rebellious man. Many believers are struggling in the workplace because of rebellion and disobedience. They would not follow simple instructions because they feel more qualified than their masters or they think they have better ideas than their masters. Some rebel because they feel their masters don't deserve their loyalty and obedience. Our obedience is not unto man but unto God. No matter how unqualified or corrupt our earthly masters may seem to us, we are commanded by God to obey them as long as we are not asked to break the commandments of God. In our workplaces, let us learn to obey our masters in the LORD and honour them in everything. There is no limit to what God can do with a man who has resolved to simply obey.

Have you found yourself in a totally corrupt and wicked workplace? Like Noah, if you will obey the LORD and walk closely with Him, He can use you to inspire change and influence the workplace. An obedient man, that's all He need.

Joseph - The Steward of God

Sold into slavery at the age of 17, Joseph rose from a steward in Potiphar's house to a ruler in Egypt, second only to Pharaoh in just 13 years. This is probably the most remarkable promotion in the Bible. If you desire promotion in your work, Joseph is your perfect mentor or example.

God has a perfect plan for everyone. The life of Joseph was very rough right from the beginning. We read from **Genesis 37:3-5** that his father loved him more than all his eleven brothers because he was the son of his old age. However, we learn that he was hated by his brothers for two reasons: the preferential love and attention he received from his father and his dreams which suggested that his brothers will serve him. Driven by envy, his brothers hatched a plan and sold him into Slavery for twenty pieces of silver when his father sent him to visit them in the field (**Genesis 37:28**). As a teenage boy, Joseph had no plan to become a slave in Egypt. Before he was sold into slavery, he was not even considered matured enough to work with his brothers in the field. He had absolutely no work experience. Yet, he was sold into slavery and later became a steward in the house of Potiphar, an officer of Pharaoh in Egypt. That is how Joseph landed his first job. It wasn't his dream job and he had no work experience but it was the job God offered him. What can we learn from Joseph?

First, we learn from Joseph that the LORD uses trials and suffering to prepare us for His work. The success of Joseph was preceded by untold pain and suffering as he narrated in **Genesis 40:15** *"For indeed I was stolen away out of the land of the Hebrews: and here also have I done nothing that they should put me into the dungeon."* The LORD allowed Joseph to suffer several challenges. In **Genesis 37:4**, we learn that his brothers hated him so much *"and could not speak peaceably unto him"*. It is very difficult to grow up with brothers who hate you so much they cannot speak peacefully to you. Then, he was forcefully sold into slavery innocently. As a slave in

Egypt, he was wrongly accused of attempting to rape Potiphar's wife and cast into prison. Although he suffered innocently, the LORD used the situation to bless him. In **Genesis 41:51-52** we read that *"And Joseph called the name of the firstborn Manasseh: For God, said he, hath made me forget all my toil, and all my father's house. And the name of the second called he Ephraim: For God hath caused me to be fruitful in the land of my affliction"*. Are you innocently suffering challenges and trials in your workplace? Have you been wrongly accused in your workplace? We have a God who can turn our trails into blessings.

Second, God will bless the work of our hands if we do His will. Joseph had exceptional work ethics and the LORD blessed the work of His hands. We read in **Genesis 39:2-3** *"And the LORD was with Joseph, and he was a prosperous man; and he was in the house of his master the Egyptian. And his master saw that the LORD was with him, and that the LORD made all that he did to prosper in his hand"*. Joseph, described as a prosperous man in this scripture doesn't mean he was rich in material things but rather he was successful at his job. He upheld strong biblical work principles and God blessed him. To start with, he was a hard worker. As a steward in Potiphar's house, he continued to work even when all the workers had left according to **Genesis 39:11**. In prison, he was the most hardworking prisoner as we read in **Genesis 39:22-23** *"And the keeper of the prison committed to Joseph's hand all the prisoners that were in the prison; and whatsoever they did there, he was the doer of it. The keeper of the prison looked not to any thing that was under his hand; because the LORD was with him, and that which he did, the LORD made it to prosper"*. Joseph was also a humble servant. We learn that he served his colleagues in prison according to **Genesis 40:41** *"And the captain of the guard charged Joseph with them, and he served them: and they continued a season in ward"*. He always exceeded expectations at work. Pharaoh only called him to interpret his dream in **Genesis 41:15** *"And Pharaoh said unto Joseph, I have dreamed a dream, and there is none that can interpret it: and I have heard say of thee, that thou canst understand a dream to interpret it"*. We read that he interpreted Pharaoh's dream and went ahead to propose a solution (**Genesis 41:33-36**). As believers, we should be known as hardworking and humble servants who always exceed expectation in our work.

Third, we must fear the LORD in our work. We read that, one day when Joseph was in the house alone to perform his duties, Potiphar's wife *"cast her eyes upon Joseph; and she said,*

Lie with me" (**Genesis 39:7**). We understand that Joseph rejected the offer to sleep with his master's wife and questioned "*how then can I do this great wickedness, and sin against God?*" (**Genesis 39:9**). At this time, the ten commandments were not yet given but Joseph feared God so much that he already knew that sleeping with another man's wife was an abomination and great wickedness in the sight of God (**Leviticus 18:20**). His ability to forgive his brothers who sold him into slavery further demonstrates his fear of God. In **Genesis 45:4-8** we read "*And Joseph said unto his brethren, Come near to me, I pray you. And they came near. And he said, I am Joseph your brother, whom ye sold into Egypt. Now therefore be not grieved, nor angry with yourselves, that ye sold me hither: for God did send me before you to preserve life. For these two years hath the famine been in the land: and yet there are five years, in the which there shall neither be earing nor harvest. And God sent me before you to preserve you a posterity in the earth, and to save your lives by a great deliverance. So now it was not you that sent me hither, but God: and he hath made me a father to Pharaoh, and lord of all his house, and a ruler throughout all the land of Egypt*". God-fearing people are humble and we also see that in Joseph. Pharaoh called him to interpret his dreams and said "*I have heard say of thee, that thou canst understand a dream to interpret it*" (**Genesis 41:15**) but Joseph replied Pharaoh in humility *"it is not in me: God shall give Pharaoh an answer of peace"* (**Genesis 41:16**). Therefore, when Joseph said in **Genesis 42:18** *"...for I fear God"*, he meant every word.

Fourth, our ultimate service is to win souls for the LORD and project the name of our God. Soul-winning was very important to Joseph. He capitalized on every opportunity to exalt his God before the people around him. With Potiphar's wife, he questioned *"how then can I do this great wickedness, and sin against God?"* (**Genesis 39:9**). He wanted the woman to understand that his righteousness was unto God. He didn't live to please man but to honour the LORD. He pointed the woman to his God. We read in **Genesis 40:8** *"And they said unto him, We have dreamed a dream, and there is no interpreter of it. And Joseph said unto them, Do not interpretations belong to God? tell me them, I pray you"*. Before Pharaoh, Joseph asked *"Do not interpretation belong to God?"*, pointing to the source of all power and the revealer of all secrets. In **Genesis 41:16** he answered Pharaoh and said *"it is not in me: God shall give Pharaoh an answer of peace"*. He used every opportunity to point people to his God. In our day-to-day activities and duties at work, God presents opportunities. We must use every opportunity to point people to the presence and power of God in our lives.

Finally, let us examine the remarkable promotion of Joseph from a slave boy to the ruler of Egypt at age thirty. He started as a steward and later promoted to an overseer in Potiphar's house according to **Genesis 39:4** *"And Joseph found grace in his sight, and he served him: and he made him overseer over his house, and all that he had he put into his hand"*. But just after this promotion, his master's wife tempted him and lied against him which eventually landed him in prison. In prison, he was made an overseer of the prisoners according to **Genesis 39:22** *"And the keeper of the prison committed to Joseph's hand all the prisoners that were in the prison; and whatsoever they did there, he was the doer of it"*. But compared to his previous job, many would have regarded his present position in prison as a massive demotion. In prison, Pharaoh's chief baker and butler who were also cast into the same prison had dreams which Joseph interpreted. Their dreams came to pass as interpreted and Joseph asked the chief butler to remember him but the Bible says *"Yet did not the chief butler remember Joseph, but forgat him"* (**Genesis 40:23**). He would go on to spend many years in prison. But when the time was right, Pharaoh dreamed a dream that no magician in the entire land of Egypt could interpret. Then the LORD opened the eyes of the butler and he remembered Joseph. Joseph was taken out of prison and interpreted Pharaoh's dream and proposed a solution to the impending famine. We read in **Genesis 41: 37-40** *"And the thing was good in the eyes of Pharaoh, and in the eyes of all his servants. And Pharaoh said unto his servants, Can we find such a one as this is, a man in whom the Spirit of God is? And Pharaoh said unto Joseph, Forasmuch as God hath shewed thee all this, there is none so discreet and wise as thou art: Thou shalt be over my house, and according unto thy word shall all my people be ruled: only in the throne will I be greater than thou."* He became one of the most successful overseers of Egypt but everything did not happen in a day. He was nurtured and pruned for the position. He started as a steward, promoted to a household supervisor, demoted to an overseer in prison where he spent most of his stay in Egypt before being lifted to a ruler in Egypt. Don't despise your humble beginnings and struggles, the LORD might be preparing you for something great.

We have learned that Joseph was a faithful worker in every position he found himself. He didn't murmur or complain about his circumstances. He trusted God and served faithfully in every position he found himself. We need to learn to serve God in our work faithfully even if we are not satisfied with our current position. As an overseer in prison, it was not the duty of Joseph to interpret dreams. But he saw every challenge as an opportunity to do something for God. The LORD then used the butler to introduce him to Pharaoh. Let us treat people around us with love and care and use every opportunity to introduce God to them because the LORD can use people around to bless us. In Joseph, we see that promotion comes only from God. The LORD used many people to promote Joseph but he didn't need to know anybody to get to where God wanted to position him. God is all you need to get to where He wants to place you. God can place you without the help of any man if you trust and obey Him. We read in **Psalm 75:6-7** *"For promotion cometh neither from the east, nor from the west, nor from the south. **But God** is the judge: he putteth down one, and setteth up another"*.

Daniel - The Man Who Stood with God

Nebuchadnezzar, the King of Babylon conquered the land of Judah and made away with part of the precious vessels in the house of the LORD. In **Daniel 1:2-4**, we read that King Nebuchadnezzar then requested that some special people among the prisoners of war be set aside to serve in his palace. Daniel was one of these special people who were selected to serve in the palace as we read in **verse 6** *"Now among these were of the children of Judah, Daniel, Hananiah, Mishael, and Azariah"*. As a prince in Judah, Daniel had no dream of serving another king in captivity. Yet, that is where God called him to serve. Like Joseph, Daniel didn't have the luxury to choose his career, but he accepted the call and the LORD used him mightily. From Daniel, we learn the following lessons:

As believers, we must purpose to serve God with all our hearts. Although Daniel found himself in a strange circumstance, he purposed in his heart to walk in purity before the LORD. As special trainees in the palace, the King had charged their caretakers to feed them with the King's food and wine. But Daniel purposed in his heart not to defile himself according to **Daniel 1:8** *"But Daniel purposed in his heart that he would not defile himself with the portion of the king's meat, nor with the wine which he drank: therefore he requested of the prince of the eunuchs that he might not defile himself"*. The first step to walking in holiness with the LORD is a resolve to live for God. Once Daniel took a stand for the LORD, the Bible says in **verse 9** *"Now God had brought Daniel into favour and tender love with the prince of the eunuchs"*. Many times, we are more concerned about the consequences of choosing to stand for God. Sometimes we worry about how to actually stand firm for the LORD in this world, where doing so is no longer popular. But if we just purpose in our hearts to walk in truth and purity before Him in our workplaces, He will take care of the details and the consequences. What the LORD requires is a heart that is resolved to obey Him no matter what.

We don't need to rebel against authority in our desire to stand for the LORD. We learn that Daniel's resolve was not in rebellion against authority. He spoke politely with the Eunuch in **Daniel 1:12-13** *"Prove thy servants, **I beseech thee, ten days; and let them give us pulse to eat, and water to drink. Then let our countenances be looked upon before thee, and the countenance of the children that eat of the portion of the king's meat: and as thou seest, deal with thy servants"**.* The Eunuch listened to Daniel's plea and took the risk to prove them in ten days. If Daniel rebelled against authority, the LORD wouldn't have come in to give him favour before the Eunuch. If we want to stand with God, we must honour authority. You don't need to rebel against your boss because he has given you a task that conflicts with the Word of God. You can turn him down politely in a way that the LORD will use the honour and respect to deal with his conscience, convert him or discourage him from the act. Rebelling against authority in our workplaces in a bid to stand firm for the LORD is against the word of God because every authority is instituted by God.

There is no regret in obeying God. After feeding on vegetables for ten days, Daniel and his brothers looked healthier than the rest who ate the King's fat food according to **Daniel 1:15** *"And at the end of ten days their countenances appeared fairer and fatter in flesh than all the children which did eat the portion of the king's meat"*. In **verse 20,** we read again that *"And in all matters of wisdom and understanding, that the king enquired of them, he found them ten times better than all the magicians and astrologers that were in all his realm"*. They were not found ten times better because they were the smartest people among the group. The LORD proved Himself mighty in them because they obeyed Him. We don't need to worry about the consequences when we stand for the LORD in our workplaces. When we are confronted with situations that are contrary to sound Biblical doctrine, we can trust God to respond mightily if we stand for Him and do what is right in His sight. If God allows the consequences to come upon us, it is for a good reason. All His ways are good and if we trust Him fully, we will never regret doing so.

Every challenge in the workplace presents a unique opportunity to witness for the LORD. In **Daniel 2**, we read that Nebuchadnezzar the King had a dream that no wise man in the land could interpret. This angered the King. He declared that all the wise men, magicians and astrologers in the entire land of Babylon should be killed. Daniel and his brothers were to be destroyed with the rest of the wise men, magicians and astrologers if no interpreter was found. We learn that Daniel went to Arioch, the captain of the King's guard who was tasked to implement the King's decision and asked for more time to interpret the dream. Daniel, Shadrach, Meshach, and Abednego prayed and asked God to intervene so that they don't perish with the heathen wise men of Babylon. The LORD answered their prayer and revealed the dream and interpretation to Daniel in a vision. When Daniel went in to interpret the dream, we read in **Daniel 2:7-28** *"Daniel answered in the presence of the king, and said, The secret which the king hath demanded cannot the wise men, the astrologers, the magicians, the soothsayers, shew unto the king;* **But there is a God in heaven that revealeth secrets, and maketh known to the king Nebuchadnezzar what shall be in the latter days...".* We see that Daniel used the challenge to introduce his God to the King. He said *"there is a God in heaven that revealeth secrets"*. Are you faced with a seemingly impossible challenge in your workplace? Probably, it is the best opportunity to witness for God if you would stand in and take the challenge for the LORD.

When authority make decisions that conflict with the Word of God, we must choose to stand with the LORD. In Daniel 3, we read that Nebuchadnezzar the king made a golden image and demanded that at the sound of some musical instruments, everyone must fall down and worship the golden image which the King had made. The consequences of defying the King's decree is clearly spelt out in **Daniel 3:6** *"And whoso falleth not down and worshippeth shall the same hour be cast into the midst of a burning fiery furnace"*. However, to worship the King's golden image will amount to breaking the commandment of God in **Exodus 20:4-5** *"Thou shalt not make unto thee any graven image, or any likeness of any thing that is in heaven above, or that is in the earth beneath, or that is in the water under the earth. Thou shalt not bow down thyself to them, nor serve them: for I the Lord thy God am a jealous God, visiting the iniquity of the fathers upon the children unto the third and fourth generation of them that hate me"*. This is a clear example of a situation where authority directly conflicts the Word of God. Shadrach, Meshach, and Abednego resolved to obey God and refused to bow down to the golden image.

The King was informed and these three Hebrew men were hauled before him and threatened with death in a burning fiery furnace. Still, they refused to worship the golden image. The angry King commanded that they should be thrown into the furnace which was heated seven times more. But the LORD delivered them from the hands of the King. They decided to obey the Word of God rather than obey the decree of the king and God delivered them from the consequences and promoted them. We must fear God rather than men because **Proverbs 29:25** says *"The fear of man bringeth a snare: but whoso putteth his trust in the LORD shall be safe"*. True safety can only be found in the will of God. We are to honour authority. But when authority push us to disobey God, we must stand firm with God.

We should always strive to exceed expectations in our work. In **Daniel 4,** we learn that the King yet again had a terrible dream and called upon Daniel to give an interpretation as no wise man in the land could interpret the dream. In **Daniel 4:24-26,** he interpreted the dream. He was only called to interpret the dream. If he did exactly that, the King would have been pleased. He wasn't going to earn any extra rewards for providing extra services. Yet, like Joseph, he exceeded expectations by not only interpreting the dream but also counselling the king according to **verse 27** "*Wherefore, O king, let my counsel be acceptable unto thee, and break off thy sins by righteousness, and thine iniquities by shewing mercy to the poor; if it may be a lengthening of thy tranquillity*". We must always strive to exceed expectation in our duties because we work for the LORD who demands perfection.

We must strive to be blameless in our work. In **Daniel 6,** we learn that King Darius set a hundred and twenty princes over the kingdom of Babylon. These princes were to report to three presidents, among whom Daniel was first. In **Daniel 6:3** we read that Daniel was preferred above the rest of the presidents. This displeased the princes and the two presidents who sought to find fault in Daniel to implicate him. But Daniel was so blameless in his work that they couldn't find a single offence against him according to **verse 4** "*Then the presidents and princes sought to find occasion against Daniel concerning the kingdom; but they could find none occasion nor fault; forasmuch as he was faithful, neither was there any error or fault found in him*". The only way they could get to him was to tempt him to disobey God according to **verse 5** "*Then said these men, We shall not find any occasion against this Daniel, except we find it against him concerning the law of his God*". If our enemies want to implicate us at work, would they find an occasion to do so? Would they find offence in the way we deliver our services, the way we treat people, our sense of diligence, professionalism, faithfulness with money, punctuality, loyalty, and other demands of our work? The LORD demands that we be blameless in our work as we are commanded in **Philippians 2:15** *"That ye may be blameless and harmless, the sons of God, without rebuke, in the midst of a crooked and perverse nation, among whom ye shine as lights in the world;"*.

We must not allow the enemy to dictate how we serve our God. In **Daniel 6:7-9** a decree was made that for the next thirty days, no one could worship any God apart from the king and anyone who flout this statute would be cast into the lion's den. The enemies knew that this was the only way they could get Daniel to break the King's law. But in **verse 10** the Bible says *"Now when Daniel knew that the writing was signed, he went into his house; and his windows being open in his chamber toward Jerusalem, he kneeled upon his knees three times a day, and prayed, and gave thanks before his God, as he did aforetime."* Daniel did not hide to worship God in fear of the decree. He knew that the King had signed the decree into law but he went into his house and opened his windows, kneeled upon his knees three times daily and prayed to the

LORD as he always did. Nothing, not even death in a lion's den could deter Daniel from worshipping God. Are you afraid to declare your faith because you might lose your job? In **Luke 9:26** the LORD said *"For whosoever shall be ashamed of me and of my words, of him shall the Son of man be ashamed, when he shall come in his own glory, and in his Father's, and of the holy angels"*.

Make prayer a habit. In **Daniel 6:10** the Bible says Daniel *"...kneeled upon his knees three times a day, and prayed, and gave thanks before his God, **as he did aforetime"***. Great men pray and powerful men are prayerful men. Clearly, Daniel was a man of prayer who revered God. He kneeled down and prayed three times daily. It is not old-fashioned to kneel in prayer. It is said that those who kneel before God can stand before any man. God deserves that reverence. Our LORD Jesus kneeled down in prayer (**Luke 22:41**). Stephen the Martyr, before he was stoned kneeled and prayed in **Acts 7:60**. When Peter the Apostle raised the dead, he kneeled down in prayer according to **Acts 9:40**. In **Acts 20:36** we read that Paul the Apostle kneeled down in prayer. We read about King Solomon in **1 Kings 8:54** *"And it was so, that when Solomon had made an end of praying all this prayer and supplication unto the LORD, he arose from before the altar of the LORD, from* *kneeling on his knees with his hands spread up to heaven.*" Ezra, the scribe kneeled down in prayer according to **Ezra 9:5**. Moses fell on his face before the LORD on several occasions and the list is inexhaustible. God did not answer the prayers of these great men because they kneeled before Him. They didn't kneel down in prayer because of fear that their prayers might not be answered. They kneeled freely before the Almighty God in all humility because He is the LORD who deserves all reverence. Come! Let us heed to the call of the Psalmist in **Psalm 95:6** "*O come, let us worship and bow down: let us kneel before the LORD our maker*".

Nehemiah - The Man who Led for God

Although leadership comes with responsibility and higher accountability, leaders have more opportunities to influence the workplace for God. This makes leadership an honour but also a challenging task to lead for God in our workplaces.

Thankfully, the Bible has the best leadership principles and mentors. The Word of God teaches clear principles of leadership that have stood the test of time. More so, the Bible contains the greatest leaders of all time. One of the less known but effective leaders in the Bible is Nehemiah. He was an ordinary man, called from captivity and sent to lead the remnant in Judah to rebuild the broken walls of

Jerusalem. In 52 days, he led a charge to complete the rebuilding, recording one of the remarkable works in history. In this section, we examine some of the Biblical leadership principles deployed by Nehemiah, after the captivity, to lead the remnants to rebuild the walls of Jerusalem and return the people back to God.

We learn from Nehemiah that God can use any man to lead, if his heart is right. Nehemiah was a captive in Persia, working as a cupbearer in the palace of Shushan. He had no leadership experience, neither was he initially called by God to lead the Jews. But he loved God and his people. One day, he inquired about the welfare of the remnants who were left of the captivity and the state of Jerusalem from certain men of Judah who were visiting the palace. When he heard that the remnants were in great affliction and that the walls of Jerusalem were broken down and the gates burned with fire, he was devastated. In **Nehemiah 1:4** he said *"And it came to pass, when I heard these words, that I sat down and wept, and mourned certain days, and fasted, and prayed before the God of heaven"*. The welfare of the remnant and Jerusalem was not his responsibility but he loved God and had a burden for the people of God. We read that when he heard the news, he wept and fasted and prayed for several days, confessing their sins and pleading on behalf of Israel for God to intervene. During the prayer and fasting, the LORD granted him favour in the sight of the King. The LORD then burdened his heart with the responsibility to go and lead the remnants to rebuild the walls of the city of God. He did not ask God to make him a leader. The first requirement of a good leader is a heart burdened with love for God and the people he seeks to lead. If we want to lead for the LORD in the workplace, we must first develop the right heart towards God and the work.

Leaders who achieve great things for God are men of prayer. When Nehemiah learned about the state of Jerusalem, we read that, he wept, fasted and humbled himself before the LORD in prayer. If we want to lead for God, we must learn to pray. Effective prayer is not about man trying twist the arm of God. Nehemiah did not try to push God to do his bidding. He humbled himself before the LORD in prayer and pleaded on behalf of himself and his nation in **Nehemiah 1:6** *"Let thine ear now be attentive, and thine eyes open, that thou mayest hear the prayer of thy servant, which I pray before thee now, day and night, for the children of Israel thy servants, and confess the sins of the children of Israel, which we have sinned against thee: **both I and my father's house have***

sinned". Effective prayer is not noisy prayer full of repetitive gibberish. God has no pleasure in noisy and misdirected prayers. We read in **Habakkuk 2:20** *"But the LORD is in his holy temple: let all the earth keep silence before him"*. Powerful prayer consists of man humbling himself before God to align his will to the will of God. In prayer, it is the will of God we seek; the work is not done by man. Prayer is not a war between man and his enemy as erroneously believed and practiced. If we could do the work, we wouldn't need to go to God. We go to the LORD in prayer to seek His will. If God is to do the job, it must be done according to His will. Powerful prayer stands on the Word of God. Nehemiah quoted scripture in his prayer according to **Nehemiah 1:8** *"Remember, I beseech thee, **the word that thou commandedst thy servant Moses…**"*. Faith is the key to an answered prayer. Faith simply means believing what God has already said in His Word. The surest way we can know that our request is within His will is when they align with scripture.

Leaders ought to pray before they take every decision. Nehemiah had fasted and prayed for several days to seek the face of God. But when the King asked him to make a request, he prayed again in **Nehemiah 2:4** *"Then the king said unto me, For what dost thou make request? **So I prayed to the**

God of heaven". If you can't rely on God for every decision, you can't lead for Him. You can be the CEO of a multinational company or even the president of the greatest nation on earth but if God does not lead you, it is impossible to make any impact for Him.

Leaders must take time to understand their task fully. When he arrived in Jerusalem, he didn't announce his arrival to the remnants. Jeremiah didn't tell them that he was their leader appointed by God to help them rebuild the walls of Jerusalem. He examined the challenge and tried to understand the task fully as he presented in **Nehemiah 2:11-13** *"So I came to Jerusalem, and was there three days. And I arose in the night, I and some few men with me; neither told I any man what my God had put in my heart to do at Jerusalem: neither was there any beast with me, save the beast that I rode upon. And I went out by night by the gate of the valley, even before the dragon well, and to the dung port, and viewed the walls of Jerusalem, which were broken down, and the gates thereof were consumed with fire"*. Leaders must take time to observe, listen and understand their work before they attempt to design solutions. Remember that Nehemiah was briefed about the broken walls of Jerusalem in the Palace of Shushan before he made his trip to Jerusalem. Yet, he found it necessary to see and confirm the extent of the ruins for himself. Leaders should not make decisions based on only what they've heard. Where possible, effort must be made to see the problem before a solution is proposed. We are accountable to the LORD for every decision and action and that makes it all-important to understand the task fully before attempting a solution.

Leaders must inspire their followers to follow the LORD. We learn from Nehemiah that followers want to identify with a shared vision. One of the first thing Nehemiah did to inspire his followers was to declare a shared vision, one that was important both to his course and the welfare and wellbeing of the remnant in Jerusalem. In **Nehemiah 2:17** we read *"Then said I unto them, Ye see the distress that we are in, how Jerusalem lieth waste, and the gates thereof are burned with fire: come, and let us build up the wall of Jerusalem, **that we be no more a reproach**"*. We also see that followers want to submit to credible authority. Another thing Nehemiah did to inspire his followers was to declare his source of authority. We read in **Nehemiah 2:18** *"**Then I told them of the hand of my God which was good upon me**; as also the king's words that he had spoken unto me. And they said, Let us rise up and build. So they strengthened their hands for this good work"*. He made them understand that he was working for God and since the remnant were people who feared God, they backed him up fully and committed to work with him. Throughout his leadership, we see that Nehemiah demonstrated total reliance on the authority of God. For example, when they were mocked by Sanballat, Tobiah, and Geshem, he replied in **Nehemiah 2:20** "... *The God of heaven, he will prosper us...*". If we want to lead for God, the people we are called to lead must share in His vision. We must demonstrate that God is our source of authority and that it is His work that we have been called to do. Our words, actions and deeds should demonstrate **1 Corinthians 11:1** "*Be ye followers of me, even as I also am of Christ.*"

Leaders should lead, not man-manage. Nehemiah did not try to teach the people how to build or repair walls. Actually, he had no expertise in building construction. He understood that his task was to lead. In **Nehemiah 2:17,** he invited the remnant over "*come, and let us build up the wall of Jerusalem, that we be no more a reproach*". After making the people see the hand of God in the work, in **verse 18,** they responded overwhelmingly "*...Let us rise up and build...*". In **Nehemiah 3,** we read that the people indeed rose up, shared the task among themselves and built the wall. Although he supervised the work, we don't read of him instructing the people how to do the work, nor did he take himself out of the task. He was present with them daily. The people had the skill to accomplish the task, they only needed leadership and vision and that is exactly what the LORD used him to provide. Together, they shared the task among themselves, each group building and repairing the part of the wall close to them. If we want to lead for God in the workplace, we must learn to trust people to work. Devise a strategy that uses every individual in the team and respect the ability of every worker. People learn to take responsibility when they are trusted.

Leaders must learn how to handle opposition. Anything that is worth doing will always meet opposition. If we are to lead for the LORD, we must learn how to handle the various forms of opposition that comes with the job. The book of Nehemiah is one of the few books in the Bible where we can learn to handle different forms of opposition in our workplaces. Before Nehemiah arrived in Jerusalem, some men were profiting from the ruins of the city and the affliction of the remnants. They were Sanballat the Horonite, and Tobiah the servant, the Ammonite. There are always people who take advantage of the suffering of others and unsolved problems in society. These wicked people would do anything to stop good leaders from solving problems. During Nehemiah's leadership, these wicked men attacked in about seven different but progressive ways:

1. *Distraction*: We read in **Nehemiah 2:10** *"When Sanballat the Horonite, and Tobiah the servant, the Ammonite, heard of it, **it grieved them exceedingly that there was come a man to seek the welfare of the children of Israel"**.* Initially, the enemies showed their opposition and displeasure in the form of pretentious sorrow. They wanted him to feel sorry for them and stop what he was about to do. At this stage, they didn't pose any physical threat to Nehemiah and the people, the enemies only attempted to distract them by showing that they were not happy with the work Nehemiah was about to do. Therefore, Nehemiah simply ignored them and went ahead with his work. That is how we should handle this kind of opposition. We shouldn't expect everyone to be happy with the work we do for the LORD.

2. *Discouragement*: In **Nehemiah 2:19** we read that *"But when Sanballat the Horonite, and Tobiah the servant, the Ammonite, and Geshem the Arabian, heard it, **they***

laughed us to scorn, and despised us, and said, What is this thing that ye do? will ye rebel against the king?*". After failing to distract them, they tried to discourage them. In **Nehemiah 2:20** he said *"Then answered I them, and said unto them, The God of heaven, he will prosper us; therefore we his servants will arise and build: but ye have no portion, nor right, nor memorial, in Jerusalem"*. We see that the surest way to handle discouragement is to encourage ourselves in the LORD. God is our help and strength.

3. *Hatred*: We read in **Nehemiah 4:1-3** *"But it came to pass, that when Sanballat heard that we builded the wall, he was wroth, and took great indignation, and mocked the Jews. And he spake before his brethren and the army of Samaria, and said, What do these feeble Jews? will they fortify themselves? will they sacrifice? will they make an end in a day? will they revive the stones out of the heaps of the rubbish which are burned? Now Tobiah the Ammonite was by him, and he said, Even that which they build, if a fox go up, he shall even break down their stone wall"*. Distraction and discouragement failed and the Jews went ahead to rebuild the wall. This made the enemy extremely angry and they hated them. In **verse 4-5** Nehemiah

turned to the LORD again for strength *"**Hear, O our God; for we are despised:** and turn their reproach upon their own head, and give them for a prey in the land of captivity: And cover not their iniquity, and let not their sin be blotted out from before thee: for they have provoked thee to anger before the builders"*. At this stage, the enemy was beginning to pose physical threat and they would do anything to stop the work. The work is the LORD's and this is the time to hand the enemies over to Him.

4. *Physical attack*: In **Nehemiah 4:7-8** we read that *"But it came to pass, that when Sanballat, and Tobiah, and the Arabians, and the Ammonites, and the Ashdodites, heard that the walls of Jerusalem were made up, and that the breaches began to be stopped, **then they were very wroth, And conspired all of them together to come and to fight against Jerusalem, and to hinder it"***. They planned to attack the Jews physically. Nehemiah handled this opposition in three ways. In **verse 9** he said *"**Nevertheless we made our prayer unto our God, and set a watch against them day and night,** because of them"* and in **verse 13** we read *"Therefore set I in the lower places behind the wall, and on the higher places, I even set the people after their families with their swords,*

their spears, and their bows". They prayed, watched their back and prepared to defend themselves.

5. *Scheming*: We read in **Nehemiah 6:1-2** "*Now it came to pass when Sanballat, and Tobiah, and Geshem the Arabian, and the rest of our enemies, heard that I had builded the wall, and that there was no breach left therein; (though at that time I had not set up the doors upon the gates;) **That Sanballat and Geshem sent unto me, saying, Come, let us meet together in some one of the villages in the plain of Ono. But they thought to do me mischief***". They plotted to kill Nehemiah, but being a wise man, he refused to meet with them. They sent for him five times but he refused to meet with them. We read in **Proverbs 27:6** "*...the kisses of an enemy are deceitful*".

6. *Blackmail*: In **Nehemiah 6:5-7** we read "*Then sent Sanballat his servant unto me in like manner the fifth time with an open letter in his hand; Wherein was written, **It is reported among the heathen, and Gashmu saith it, that thou and the Jews think to rebel: for which cause thou buildest the wall, that thou mayest be their king, according to these words. And thou hast also appointed prophets to preach of thee at Jerusalem, saying,***

There is a king in Judah: **and now shall it be reported to the king according to these words.** *Come now therefore, and let us take counsel together".* They tried to instil fear in him by framing a story to blackmail him. But he responded to them in **verse 8-9** *"Then I sent unto him, saying, There are no such things done as thou sayest, but thou feignest them out of thine own heart. For they all made us afraid, saying, Their hands shall be weakened from the work, that it be not done.* **Now therefore, O God, strengthen my hands".** Still, he refused to accept a meeting with them. Be wise to avoid any form of alliance with the enemy no matter what they promise.

7. *Internal Enemies*: We read in **Nehemiah 6:10** *"Afterward I came unto the house of Shemaiah the son of Delaiah the son of Mehetabeel, who was shut up; and he said, Let us meet together in the house of God, within the temple, and let us shut the doors of the temple: for they will come to slay thee; yea, in the night will they come to slay thee".* When they failed to get Nehemiah by themselves, they tried to use one of the Jews to trap him in the temple so they could kill him. But again, the wise Nehemiah responded boldly in **verse 11-12** *"And I said, Should such a man as I flee? and who is*

*there, that, being as I am, would go into the temple to save his life? I will not go in. And, lo, I perceived that God had not sent him; but that he pronounced this prophecy against me: **for Tobiah and Sanballat had hired him***". When the enemy fails to get to us direct, he will most likely use people who are closer to us.

If we want to be successful leaders for God, we must learn how to handle the various forms of opposition that come with the job. Every work of God will be opposed by physical or spiritual enemies. From Nehemiah's experience, we conclude that total reliance on God, prayer and exercise of wisdom is what we need to overcome the enemy.

Great leaders need committed followers. In **Nehemiah 4:6,** he testified about the commitment of the people "*So built we the wall; and all the wall was joined together unto the half thereof: **for the people had a mind to work***". On one hand, good leaders are made by committed and loyal followers. On the other hand, committed followers are made by inspirational leaders who care and fights for their followers. Obviously, the entire work was done by the LORD as he testified in **Nehemiah 6:16** "*And it came to pass, that when all our enemies heard thereof, and all the heathen that were about us saw these things, they were much cast down in their own eyes: **for they***

perceived that this work was wrought of our God". Yet, Nehemiah succeeded because the people had a mind to work. They stood with him through all the opposition and worked day and night to build the wall. In return, Nehemiah fought for them and took the front row when they faced opposition. We must take time to build a committed team if we want to lead successfully. If we can demonstrate love and care for our followers, they will commit to work assiduously for us.

Leaders must protect their followers. Sanballat and Tobiah had plotted to besiege the Jews in **Nehemiah 4:11** "*And our adversaries said, They shall not know, neither see, till we come in the midst among them, and slay them, and cause the work to cease*". When Nehemiah heard what Sanballat and Tobiah had plotted, he devised a formidable plan to protect the people according to **verse 13-15** "*Therefore set I in the lower places behind the wall, and on the higher places, I even set the people after their families with their swords, their spears, and their bows. And I looked, and rose up, and said unto the nobles, and to the rulers, and to the rest of the people, Be not ye afraid of them: remember the Lord, which is great and terrible, and fight for your brethren, your sons, and your daughters, your wives, and your houses. And it came to pass, when our enemies heard that it* *was known unto us, and God had brought their counsel to nought, that we returned all of us to the wall, every one unto his work"*. These are the few verses where we see Nehemiah personalise his work. Great leaders take the front row in difficult times and take the back row when the victory is won. From this scripture, we learn that he quickly designed a strategy and motivated the people to put their trust in the LORD. He worked hard to protect them from their adversary to keep the work going. We must commit ourselves to protect the people who work for us and take full responsibility for their welfare and stand for them in difficult times. That is what great leaders do.

Leaders must hate sin. Contrary to today's world where we expect leaders to be always soft and accept everything thrown at them, Nehemiah was a strong leader who loved God and hated sin. In **Nehemiah 5**, it was reported to him that some men among the Jews were taking advantage of the poor. These wicked men took the children of the poor people into slavery and seized their vineyards and houses as payment of huge interest (usury) on corn which the people borrowed to feed their families. This was against the law in **Exodus 22:25** *"If thou lend money to any of my people that is poor by thee, thou shalt not be to him as an usurer, neither shalt thou lay upon him* *usury*" and **Deuteronomy 23:19** "*Thou shalt not lend upon usury to thy brother; usury of money, usury of victuals, usury of any thing that is lent upon usury*". In **Nehemiah 5:1** we read that "*And there was a great cry of the people and of their wives against their brethren the Jews*". When Nehemiah heard these things, first, he rebuked the nobles and rulers who were taking advantage of the people according to **verses 6 and 7** "*And I was very angry when I heard their cry and these words. Then I consulted with myself, and I rebuked the nobles, and the rulers, and said unto them, Ye exact usury, every one of his brother. And I set a great assembly against them*". Second, he told them that what they have done is wrong and a sin against the LORD in **verse 9** "*Also I said, It is not good that ye do: ought ye not to walk in the fear of our God because of the reproach of the heathen our enemies?*" and third, he corrected them in **verse 11** "*Restore, I pray you, to them, even this day, their lands, their vineyards, their oliveyards, and their houses, also the hundredth part of the money, and of the corn, the wine, and the oil, that ye exact of them*". Leaders of God need to stand up and confront sin and rebuke those who refuse to do right. By rebuking them, the nobles accepted correction and walked right with God and peace returned to the Land. The ability to boldly rebuke and correct is one of the most important strengths of a great leader.

In conclusion, the ultimate goal of our leadership is to turn the people we lead to the LORD. Leaders who lead faithfully for God are often used to solve human challenges, but the ultimate goal is to lead people to the LORD. As Nehemiah led the people to rebuild the ruined walls of Jerusalem, he didn't forget this all-important objective to return the people back to God. After the wall was built, He appointed Levites priests and established worship in Jerusalem. The hearts of the people returned to God and they desired to know His commandments that they may obey the LORD their God and walk with Him as we read in **Nehemiah 8:1** *"And all the people gathered themselves together as one man into the street that was before the water gate; and they spake unto Ezra the scribe to bring the book of the law of Moses, which the Lord had commanded to Israel"*. Many things might have led to this. First, the people saw the mighty works of God according to **Nehemiah 6:16**. Second, Nehemiah led them to the LORD during challenging times (**Nehemiah 2:20, 4:4, 6:14, 7:5**). The people were led by an uncompromising man who feared God greatly and hated evil and that created a ripple effect throughout the camp. Even before Ezra started reading the book of the Law, we read in **Nehemiah 8:6** *"And Ezra blessed the Lord, the great God. And all the people answered, Amen, Amen, with lifting up their* *hands: and they bowed their heads, and worshipped the Lord with their faces to the ground"*. The fear of God had returned to the land as the people revere the LORD in humility. Finally, we see a repented nation as the people wept when the law was read to them according to **Nehemiah 8:9** *"And Nehemiah, which is the Tirshatha, and Ezra the priest the scribe, and the Levites that taught the people, said unto all the people, This day is holy unto the Lord your God; mourn not, nor weep. For all the people wept, when they heard the words of the law"*. We read in **2 Corinthians 7:10** *"For godly sorrow worketh repentance to salvation not to be repented of: but the sorrow of the world worketh death"*. The people desired to hear the law of God. They humbled themselves before the LORD in worship, some wept in regret of their sins. These are evidence of genuine repentance. The works of God and the leadership of Nehemiah worked this repentance and returned the people back to God. As God uses us to solve challenges in the workplace, we must not forget that the ultimate objective is to reconcile the people with God.

Summary

In this chapter, we examined the testimony of prominent men of God. From Noah, we learned how to obey God and authority in our work. We learned about stewardship, service and promotion from Joseph and how to stand firm for the Lord from the testimony of Daniel and the three Hebrew men, Shadrach, Meshach and Abednego. Finally, we learnt strong leadership principles from Nehemiah, an ordinary man called and prepared by God to lead the remnant of Israel to rebuild the broken walls of Jerusalem. From these remarkable testimonies, we see how the Word of God is timeless and applicable in the various aspects of our workplaces even in today's fast-changing and technology-driven workplace.

PREPARING TO WORK

"For other foundation can no man lay than that is laid, which is Jesus Christ." **1 Corinthians 3:11**

God has promised in **Malachi 3:5** *"For I am the Lord, I change not"*. We also read in **Matthew 24:35** *"Heaven and earth shall pass away, but my words shall not pass away"*. Because of these and other similar promises, we know for sure that the Word of God will always be profitable.

The doctrine for believers in the workplace has been presented in the preceding chapters. We have also seen these principles work in the lives of great men who were used by God in the Bible. However, a lot have changed. The way we work, relationships at work, mode of promotion, and rules in the workplace have all changed. The question is, can we still succeed in today's fast-paced, diverse and dynamic workplace by relying solely on these Biblical principles? YES, we strongly believe so. The Bible's way is not just one of the ways to succeed at work, it is the ONLY WAY the believer can successfully serve God in the workplace. In this chapter, we lay down the foundation for believers who aspire to build a strong career to honour the LORD in their workplaces.

The Ten Common Sins of believers in the Workplace

Many professing believers are not effective in their work. This does not mean believers are not making enough money in their work. Actually, most believers in the workplace are getting promoted, some are making huge sums of money and a lot are winning career awards. However, many haven't lived up to the standards required by the LORD in the workplace. We haven't honoured God with our work and we haven't worked according to the commandments of God in the Bible. Because we have not served God with our work, we have become ineffective in influencing our workplaces for the LORD and winning souls for Him. The reason why most of us haven't been productive for the LORD is because of these ten common sins in our workplaces:

1. *Laziness*: Most of us are working just enough to get paid. We show up at work, fulfil the minimum working conditions and find means to earn maximum pay. We don't care about our work, our employers and definitely about God in our work. We don't give our best at work and this is against

Ecclesiastes 9:10 *"Whatsoever thy hand findeth to do, do it with thy might;..."*

2. *Pride*: Many of us want to be praised and worshipped before we give our best. We would do everything to sabotage people who don't bow to our demands. Many of us wouldn't provide satisfactory services unless clients offer maximum respect. But we are stewards called to serve. Nothing, but humble stewards. Pride in the workplace is contrary to **Matthew 20:27-28** *"And whosoever will be chief among you, let him be your servant: Even as the Son of man came not to be ministered unto, but to minister, and to give his life a ransom for many."*

3. *Greed*: Many of us work because of money. It is not wrong to earn money from your work. But it is sinful to work for the sole reason of earning money to gain material wealth contrary to **Proverbs 23:4** *"Labour not to be rich: cease from thine own wisdom"*. For this reason, some of us have become covetous to the point that we would do anything to earn more money contrary to the admonition by the **LORD** in **Luke 12:15** *"...Take heed, and beware of covetousness: for a*

man's life consisteth not in the abundance of the things which he possesseth".

4. ***Theft***: Unfortunately, stealing is becoming an accepted norm in our society. Stealing work time, money and other resources for personal gain, demanding additional remuneration for tasks we have been paid to fulfil and taking bribes, all amounts to theft. The Christian worker is a big culprit of these forms of stealing, especially short-changing people. Stealing of any form is a sin as it is against **Leviticus 19:11** "*Ye shall not steal, neither deal falsely, neither lie one to another.*"

5. ***Iniquity***: Many believers in the workplace treat people according to their outward appearance and personality. We tend to play nice towards people who appear rich and act rude towards those who appear poor. We favour friends, close kinsmen and family and act indifferent towards people we don't know. The sin of treating people unjustly is called iniquity and the LORD hates it as we read in **Proverbs 11:1** "*A false balance is abomination to the LORD: but a just weight is his delight.*"

6. *Scheming*: Finding means other than diligence to attain favour or promotion. Many Christian workers have been involved in sinful deals to earn a job and in an attempt to get themselves promoted. Many have paid bribes, committed sexual sins, awarded contracts to wrong people, and covered crime in an attempt to get ahead at work. Scheming is a sin and against **Proverbs 3:7** *"Be not wise in thine own eyes: fear the LORD, and depart from evil"*.

7. *Wickedness*: Many believers are simply wicked in the workplace. We don't have feelings for the circumstances of clients, we don't care about the welfare of the employer, we have no respect for time and we don't care about the consequences of our decisions as long as the pay cheque is not affected. There have been many cases where market women use poisonous adulterants to increase sales margin. These forms of behaviour in our workplaces are pure wickedness and the LORD hates it as we read in **Proverbs 21:27** *"The sacrifice of the wicked is abomination: how much more, when he bringeth it with a wicked mind?"*

8. *Unprofessionalism*: Many believers are unable to separate professional work from personal affairs. It is shameful that many of us can't work with people we don't agree with at the personal level. We play during work and work when it is time to play. The CEO would not promote a diligent worker he disagrees with. These are just a few forms of unprofessionalism at work. We are commanded in **Ephesians 6:6-7** to work *"Not with eyeservice, as menpleasers; but as the servants of Christ, doing the will of God from the heart; With good will doing service, as to the Lord, and not to men."*

9. *Lawlessness*: Many believers still need strict supervision to perform their tasks. We can't be trusted to act responsibly in the absence of our supervisors. We can't be trusted with money, time, information, responsibility and initiative. We are lawless people who have no respect for authority, rule of law and regulations contrary to **Ephesians 6:5** *"Servants, be obedient to them that are your masters according to the flesh, with fear and trembling, in singleness of your heart, as unto Christ;"*.

10. *Ignorance*: Many believers stop learning the moment they find a job. We lack lifelong learning skills and are therefore unable to cope with the fast-changing workplace. This leads to mediocre work. Some of us are not teachable; we often lack the humility to learn from people. Ignorance at work is a sin because it brings shame and disrepute to the name of the LORD. We are commanded to study to meet the standard required for effective work in our positions according to **2 Timothy 2:15** *"Study to shew thyself approved unto God, a workman that needeth not to be ashamed..."*

A Great Opportunity

Job opportunities are very limited and they keep dwindling by the day. Employers are hunting for skilled workers with impeccable attitudes to fill the limited positions. Talent abounds everywhere and many believers in the working class are highly educated and skilled in their field of work. Therefore, it is not difficult to find talent in many fields of work. In areas where talent is scarce, many employers will compromise on talent and skills if the candidate is teachable. However, it is becoming increasingly hard to find gifted workers with the right attitude and many employers will hardly compromise on attitude. It is safe to predict that over 90% of believers commit the ten common sins discussed in the preceding section, making many of them unemployable in an ideal position. The remaining 10% of workers who may have acceptable attitudes are in high demand, regardless of the scarcity of jobs in the country. On the surface, it may seem that every job position in the country is filled. But on the other hand, no employer is happy with his employees. Many employers will fire their workers if they are guaranteed workers with better attitudes.

As unemployment increases across the globe, believers who will commit to serve the LORD with their career will fall in the top 1% of workers in high demand. Believers who honour God in their work have the best attitude as they strive to please God who demands nothing but excellence. They have the best motivation, respect for authority, productivity, endurance, loyalty, faithfulness and stewardship. Also, we have the Holy Spirit who works in us to develop humanly impossible attitudes at work. Above all, we have a God who blesses the work of our hands when we work lawfully and strive to honour Him with our work.

Understanding Employment

We are not interested in detailed technical definitions. We want to devise comprehensive definitions that are practical and suitable to the Biblical principles of work presented in this book. Generally, we may identify four main types of employment:

1. *Overemployment*: Working more than we can offer in terms of skills and time. This includes workers who have been placed in positions higher than their actual qualification. A rather exaggerated example is a high school graduate with no work experience, employed as the branch manager of a bank. This worker for example is overemployed in terms of his skill set. Workers who work too many hours a week in different jobs that require different sets of skills are overemployed in terms of time. For example, a full-time teacher who also runs a supermarket, owns a farm and drives a taxi. All these four jobs require time and a different set of skills. The advantage is the multiple sources of income. But there are several disadvantages. First, because his attention is divided over several jobs, it is difficult to master any of the jobs. He becomes a jack of all trades, master of none. Lack of mastery in any of the jobs means he may

struggle to become very good at any of the jobs. Second, working for too many hours a day leaves him with no time to sharpen his skills and develop new skills. In today's fast-changing workplaces, the inability to learn new skills and adapt to new ways of working will stunt your growth and eventually make you redundant. If you are overemployed in terms of time, reduce your workload to a maximum of 12 hours a day, 6 days a week. You may work two or more different jobs as long as the jobs require similar sets of skills so that you can develop these skills and master them properly. Focus on the Key Performance Indicators (KPIs) and trust the LORD to reward your faithfulness. Working several different jobs increases your earnings temporarily but you only get ahead by mastering a skill and getting promoted. If you are overemployed in terms of skills, invest more time to develop your skills to the required standard so that you can be a *"workman that needeth not to be ashamed"*. If the skills gap is too wide, it is advisable to quit and move to a job that matches your current skills. We can't serve God effectively in a position where we are not qualified to work because our inefficiencies will bring disrepute to the name of the LORD.

2. *Employment*: Working a job that matches your skills and time. This means you are working with your maximum skill set, paid according to your qualification and output and the work provides a clear path for promotion and lifelong learning. Per this definition, if you are a trained mason who is working as a labourer at a construction site for 8 hours a day, 6 days a week, you have a job but you are not employed. If you are a trained teacher who needs 8 working hours a day to make a living but your current job can only offer 4 working hours a day, you are not fully employed. If you are a trained engineer, working in a position that matches your skills and offers you maximum working hours but the job doesn't give you the opportunity to develop your skills and get promoted, you are not fully employed. If you have developed your skills or acquired more skills to the point where you are working below your skill set, you are no longer employed.

3. *Underemployment*: Working less than you can offer in terms of skills and time. It means you work less

than the number of hours you actually want to work, using less skills than you actually possess. This also include those who have outgrown their current position and workers who are paid less than the market value of their qualification and output. Per the definition, if you are a trained teacher who works as a taxi driver, you are underemployed, regardless of your earnings. If you have time for full-time employment but has only been offered a part-time job, you are underemployed. If you are a graduate teacher who earns less than your market value, you are underemployed. If you are underemployed, dedicate your work to God by working in accordance to the doctrine and principles outlined in the early chapters. Invest more time to develop valuable skills and avoid the temptation to work several jobs at a time. The LORD can use the same position to promote you or open another door that will utilize your new skillset. There is always a prepared place for a prepared person. If you will accept your current position, honour the LORD with it and develop yourself, God will open the door.

4. *Unemployment:* You have no job at all. This means you are not working because you can't find anything

to do. Per this definition, to be unemployed is a sin against God because we are commanded in **Ecclesiastes 9:10** *"Whatsoever thy hand findeth to do, do it with thy might..."*. The Bible says "whatsoever" your hands find to do. Everyone can find something to do for a living. For example, you can work as a labourer at a construction site, in the farm, helping people in the market for a fee, weeding etc. To sit home doing nothing is a sin. If you are unemployed, go out there and get yourself underemployed. This means finding a job below your skills and available working time. It takes a lot of courage and humility but if you take the steps to obey God, He will open doors. You might not stay underemployed for long before the right door is opened. The LORD has promised that if we are faithful in the little, He will entrust us with more. Everyone admires the humility of a graduate who doesn't mind working as a labourer at a construction site. It shows your determination to succeed and your humility to serve. You might not need the money but if you take a low-level job simply because God doesn't approve unemployment, He will honour you in return.

Preparing for a Great Career

A lot of preparation goes into a successful career, especially one that seeks to bring honour to the name of the LORD. Therefore, it is very important to plan and prepare adequately for the task ahead. The LORD asked in **Luke 14:28** *"For which of you, intending to build a tower, sitteth not down first, and counteth the cost, whether he have sufficient to finish it?"*. We are also counselled in **Proverbs 24:17** *"Prepare thy work without, and make it fit for thyself in the field; and afterwards build thine house"*. However, it is equally important to understand that our hope for a successful career is not anchored on our preparations but on our God. We prepare simply because God requires it. In **Proverbs 21:31** we read that *"The horse is prepared against the day of battle: but safety is of the LORD"*. It is important to prepare the horse against the day of battle but equally necessary to know that safety is of the LORD. This is in contrast with the popular false teaching that "God helps those who help themselves". By preparing adequately, we are not trying to help ourselves so God can help us. The LORD doesn't need the help of man to accomplish His will. We prepare because He commands it, not because we want to help Him to help us. That is very important so that we don't share in the glory of God.

Without Him, we can do nothing. In this section, we discuss some basic requirements for a great career.

Acquiring a Skill

Skill training is the first requirement for a successful career. Acquiring a skill is more than just obtaining a certificate or qualification. With the structure of our modern education system, it is possible to graduate with a degree or even a doctorate degree without necessarily mastering the requisite skills. Definitely, one can find a job with such certificates, but he can't fulfil a career and make the right impact for the LORD without the requisite skills. To work for the LORD in our workplaces, first of all, we need to be skilled at what we do.

The most valuable skill in the 21st century and beyond is the exceptional ability to identify a skill gap, learn, master and implement new skills to solve problems. Even the most gifted students cannot exhaust all the skills they will need in future, no matter the number of years they spend in school or in training. The 21st century workplace is technology-driven and changes at a remarkable pace. Constantly, new skills are required to improve existing solutions and tackle emerging challenges. The workers who will succeed in this system are those who have mastered the art and science of learning and implementing new skills faster on the job. Unfortunately, self-education is not taught in schools. Therefore, the Christian worker should be prudent to train himself into a fast learner in his field of work. Here are a few ideas for skills acquisition.

The skills we choose to master should be in tandem with our innate gifts. God has given every man a gift of talent. For example, by dint of hard work, everyone can study to become a teacher, but a gifted teacher is exceptional. Two criteria should guide our choice of skills to master for a career. First, what we do must make use of our innate gifts. God put those gifts in us to use them for His service. Second, what we do must be good in the sight of God because the LORD only gives good gifts according to **James 1:17** *"Every good gift and every perfect gift is from above, and cometh down from the Father of lights, with whom is no variableness, neither shadow of turning"*. For example, one cannot say he is a gifted thief or liar. Such are not giftings no matter how much they pay. However, if you have built a career in an area that doesn't use most of your innate gifts, you don't necessarily need to change your career. It has been shown that people who are exceptionally good at what they do can find fulfilment in their work. Like Joseph and Daniel, accept your career and invest time to perfect your skills. If you dedicate your career to the LORD, He will give you fulfilment as you strive to perfect your work to serve Him.

We must take our time to master the skill. Formal education is good and most people acquire their skills from school. However, self-education can equally be used to perfect a skill. Actually, many exceptionally gifted people are self-taught. With abundance of materials and free courses on the internet, we can master any skill. Apprenticeship is another effective way to learn a skill directly from a master. The mode of skills acquisition depends on the type of skill we want to acquire and the resources available at our disposal. However, a lot of patience and diligence are required to master any skill.

We must know when we have mastered a skill. The criterion of mastery is when we can put our lives on the line for our work. For example, as a trained teacher, you have mastered your skill if you will be happy when all teachers who teach your own children are skilled exactly like you. As a trained medical doctor, you have mastered your skill if you would be comfortable when the doctor who attends to you on your sick bed is skilled exactly like you. As a mason, would you confidently build your own house? As a carpenter, would you trust yourself with all the carpentry needs of your house? Sharpen your skills until you can put yourself on the line for your work. That is only when you can trust that you've mastered your trade.

We must focus more on universal or transferable skills. In every field of work, there are transferable skills. These are skills we can take with us to any place of work. For example, document preparation skills, developing presentations, computer programming, teaching skills, universal problem-solving techniques, research skills, writing skills, people skills, listening skills, organisational skills, team skills, etc. These skills transcend professions and their value only increases with time. In critical times, some of these transferable skills can earn us a job in another field. People who have exceptional transferable skills also widen their job opportunities because they tend to require minimum training to fit into several positions.

Finding a Job

We have discussed some criteria for choosing a job. A believer can work in any company to earn a living but he can't serve God in every company. For example, we can't honour God with our work if we work in a brewery that produces alcoholic drinks. God will not use your work if you run a nightclub. A medical doctor who conducts abortion procedures certainly doesn't honour God. God will only use our work if it serves His will. The career we choose must not flout the Word of God.

Given the fierce competition for jobs, what is the best way to find a job today? In the past, finding a job was straightforward; you acquire a skill, prepare a CV, search for a job advertisement, apply for the job, attend an interview and hopefully get hired. That is fast becoming obsolete. Presently, a lot of companies are hiring but they hardly advertise vacant job positions. Sometimes, the vacancy is already taken even before the job is advertised. Therefore, waiting to respond to an advertised job vacancy may be just too late. We must find a better way to sell our skills to potential employers. We identify three effective ways to find a job, especially in the private sector:

1. *By recommendation*: Most HR managers and hiring agents consult people in their network before they advertise positions. They speak to people in their network to recommend proven talent for them to hire. Some of the people they consult include other HR managers, managers in other companies, faculty of institutions, and other trusted colleagues. This

makes it all important to build a strong network. Everyone we meet is a potential lead to our next job. Use every opportunity to discuss your needs, skill set and ambition with people in your network, they may know people who are hiring.

2. ***By marketing your skills***: Prepare a short video of your major projects, highlighting your exceptional skills and qualities and share the video on relevant social media platforms. This is not the time to present your certificates, degrees, education and achievements. That wouldn't go far. We mean videos showing real practical works you have done. If you are a teacher, we want to see how you teach. If you are a mason, we want to see you lay some blocks, do some plastering etc. If you are a nurse, we want to see you at work. Thanks to smartphones and the internet, this type of pitching can be done with ease. Upload the video on social media, for example LinkedIn and share with potential employers. If you have perfected your skills, the video will definitely go viral and increase your chances of landing a job.

3. ***By solving a real problem***: You may also land a job if you can identify a pressing need in a company and

propose a viable solution to the problem. Identify your potential employers, study their operations and identify potential ways of improving their services. Prove that the solutions you are proposing are plausible and show how it cuts down cost, increases profit, reduces environmental footprint or helps them beat competition. Draft your solution into a proposal and pitch your work in a three-minute video presentation. Mail your work to the HR manager, CEO or other key stakeholders of the company. You may earn at least an interview if your proposal is compelling.

These proposed ways of finding jobs do not write off the need to develop traditional job application skills. Valuable job application skills such as CV preparation, writing a compelling cover letter, job interview skills, and proposal writing skills are important for several reasons. First, many companies still demand them for employment, especially public institutions. Second, they are transferable soft skills that can be applied in several other aspects of work. Third, a lot of learning go into perfecting these skills and every learning process is profitable. Finally, the process of preparing these documents compels us to think through our skills, look at what we can really offer, and learn to communicate the exact value of our skills in a way that will convince the employer. This helps us to develop indispensable pitching skills to market ourselves, acquiring marketing skills that can be transferred to other areas of work.

What about those who want to move into a new role in their workplaces? Several factors may compel a worker to apply for a vacant position within the company; promotion, higher salary, a more interesting project, desire for a new working environment, to join a more compatible team, etc. These are all good reasons to apply for another job in a company. However, believers who want to apply for internal positions should be guided by the following principles:

a. *Seek the consent of your boss*: If the position was not recommended by your boss, seek his consent before you apply. The hiring manager will definitely speak to your boss before you are hired. In addition, loyalty to your current boss is an indication that your new boss can rely on you. Also, knowing that you will need the recommendation of your boss to move to any position within or outside the company helps you to relate well with him. If your boss doesn't support your application, don't apply for the position.

b. *Discuss your intention with your potential boss*: Speak with the hiring manager and the boss you will be working for if you are hired in the new role. Discuss your ambition and skill set with them and seek their sincere opinion about your chances of working with them. Many times, the boss will open up to you if you don't meet their requirements. He might encourage you to apply but from his conversation you can evaluate your chances of getting hired. If they don't approve your application, don't apply for the position because probably it was created with someone in mind.

c. *Develop a rapport with the team you want to work with*: spend your breaks to hang out with colleagues who work for that team even before a vacant position is announced. Show your readiness to learn more about the new role. Do some extra learning and share ideas with them. Volunteer to help them on tasks where they might need additional hands during your free time. Identify solutions to their challenges if you can. The next time a position is vacant, you might be the first person to know about it and the team will recommend you to the boss as a good fit. Do this without compromising on the time you spend on your current job.

Whether we are hunting for a fresh job or seeking to move into a new role, we must allow the LORD to lead us. We must be guided by **Proverbs 3:6** *"In all thy ways acknowledge him, and he shall direct thy paths"*. The LORD will not choose a job for us, but He will lead us into the right one if we allow Him. If we want to work for Him, it is only fit to allow Him to place us where He has purposed for us to serve.

Time Management

It is often said that time is money. But in reality, time is more than money because whiles we can use our time to make money, no amount of money can buy us more than 24 hours a day. Time is fixed, everyone has a daily account of 24 hours. The difference between success and failure is in how we use our time.

What does the Bible teach about time? Probably the most popular scriptures about time are **Ecclesiastes 3:1** *"To every thing there is a season, and a time to every purpose under the heaven."* and **Ecclesiastes 9:11** *"I returned, and saw under the* *sun, that the race is not to the swift, nor the battle to the strong, neither yet bread to the wise, nor yet riches to men of understanding, nor yet favour to men of skill; but time and chance happeneth to them all*". From these scriptures, we can learn a lot about time including the following:

1. ***God provides enough time for His purpose***: We often complain that we don't have enough time to work and serve the LORD. But we read that God has provided "*a time to every purpose under the heaven*". Every day, the LORD provides enough time to fulfil every task He assigns to us. However, God does not provide time for wastage. For every wasted time, we lose a valuable time to fulfil God's will. If we seem to be struggling to make enough time for essential things in our lives, most often, it is because we are wasting time on less important things. If we allow the LORD to lead us daily, we will always find enough time to work for Him.

2. ***Everyone is given enough time to be successful***: Our generous LORD does not only provide enough time for all His works; He also gives everyone the same measure of time daily. We read that "*time and chance*" happens to everyone. The LORD has made a just

provision of time for everyone to succeed. Believers who will learn to use this valuable resource wisely, will succeed. People who waste time on useless ventures, struggle to get important things done.

3. *Time should be planned*: The scripture *"To every thing there is a season"* implies that each task should be accomplished at an appointed time. Therefore, the 24-hour daily account should be apportioned to meet the various needs of the day. The LORD opens each day with various responsibilities spread throughout the day. It is our duty to seek Him and find what He wants us to do each day, when He wants them done and then apportion the time wisely to meet the demands of each task fully. Therefore, for the believer, time management actually means seeking the will of God for each time of the day and striving to fulfil it.

4. *There is no free time*: God doesn't provide free time. This doesn't mean we can't spend time to rest and engage in a leisure or hobby. Rest is very important to the plans of God as we will learn later. However, we are accountable to God for how we use our time daily according to **Romans 14:12** *"So then every one of*

us shall give account of himself to God". Therefore, even our leisure time should be deliberately planned to fit into the will of God.

From these scriptures, we learn that, each day, God assigns the believer duties and the required time to get each task done. Simply put, God has a daily timetable for every child of His. All we are required to do is to follow His timetable. Therefore, the most important task for the believer as far as time is concerned is to find the will of God for every time of the day and follow it through.

Using Time Wisely

The believer has a maximum of six working days a week as commanded in **Exodus 20:9** "*Six days shalt thou labour, and do all thy work*". We do not believe that the believer is commanded to observe the Sabbath as written in the Law. The Sabbath was specifically given to the Children of Israel according to **Exodus 31:16** "*Wherefore the children of Israel shall keep the sabbath, to observe the sabbath throughout their generations, for a perpetual covenant*". However, if God worked for six days and commanded the Jews to work for six days, then it is good to work for six days. It is advisable that the believer should not work for money on the day of worship. Not working at all on worship days gives us maximum concentration during Church service and provides ample time for family fellowship and Bible study after Church. Finally, honouring God with one full day out of seven is a worthy service. God deserves at least a full day out of the seven He has freely given to us.

We shall divide the daily 24-hour account into three parts, 8 hours each called **Service**, **Renewal** and **Rest** time.

Service Time: It is within the will of God that every believer should work for six days a week. In these six days, we can spend 8 hours daily to work. A day's job often requires us to work from morning (6 - 9 am) to evening (4-6 pm), depending on the nature of the job. The demands of a night job may vary significantly depending on the nature of the work. At least, we know that God approves the use of time to work. Although the amount of time we spend at work may vary from person to person, depending on where the LORD has positioned us to serve, we know that it is the will of God, that each day, every believer uses part of the time given to him to work.

Renewal Time: God has also assigned us daily family duties. We can dedicate about 8 hours a day to fulfil this purpose, which includes, leading and protecting the family, spending time with our spouses, raising children, teaching the family the Word of God, family outings and fellowships and other family needs. The LORD also commands us to study (**1 Timothy 4:13; 2 Timothy 2:15**). Therefore, a part of our renewal time (say 2 hours daily) should be dedicated to personal study and growth. This includes a personal devotion to study the Word of God and professional studies where we engage in lifelong learning to pick up useful skills applicable to our work. If we are not studying the Bible daily and we seem to lack time to pick relevant professional skills or read some useful books, then it is because we have wasted the time provided by God for daily studies. Daily studies are important part of our renewal time. The renewal time also includes the time we spend to exercise our bodies and engage in activities that keep us healthy. These are all things we know the LORD approves and commands us to do daily.

Rest Time: We read in the book of Genesis that God rested on the seventh day after creation. Does God need rest? Definitely no, He doesn't need rest. We believe He rested to demonstrate the importance of rest after work. In **Mark 6:31** our LORD Jesus Christ said to His disciples "...*Come ye yourselves apart into a desert place, and rest a while: for there were many coming and going, and they had no leisure so much as* *to eat*". In this scripture, the LORD demonstrated the need to rest after work. Therefore, it is the will of God that we rest daily after work. It has been demonstrated that 8 hours of sleep is enough for the body. A healthy adult may not need 8 hours of sleep but sleep is not the only form of rest. Rest also includes leisure time when we engage in hobbies that take our attention from work and family duties. Every hard worker needs a lot of rest after work to recover fully for the next day's activities.

The practice of apportioning the daily account of time into three parts is very useful but the 8 hours is not a rule. Some workers may need less time at work and more time with family. Some require more time at work and less time with family. We can work out the time to fit our daily needs as directed by the LORD. God has a unique plan for every child of His.

Dealing with Procrastination

It is often said that procrastination is the thief of time. In **John 9:4,** the LORD said "*I must work the works of him that sent me, while it is day: the night cometh, when no man can work*". In this scripture, the LORD demonstrated that we need to work with a high sense of urgency. Procrastination waste time and makes us inefficient, untrustworthy and miserable. We must train ourselves to work with a high sense of urgency in everything we do so that we use the time provided by God efficiently.

Learning to be Punctual

Nothing destroys the testimony of a believer more than lateness. We must always be punctual in every aspect of our lives because it is the measure of our competence and dependability. Being punctual shows that we are competent. It shows we have control over our time and we can be dependable and trusted with the time of others. Habitual late commers cannot be trusted with time. Lateness shows disrespect for other people contrary to **Philippians 2:4** *"Look not every man on his own things, but every man also on the things of others"*. The following are recommended to improve punctuality:

    a. **Understand punctuality:** Punctuality literarily means respecting the time of others. When we accept an appointment, we are automatically entrusted with the time of all the people involved in the program. Showing up at meetings late steals time from all these people who are trusting us with their time. Lateness is theft. We steal the time of people when we can't keep appointments. We are stealing time from our employers when we show up at work late. Theft of every form is sin against the LORD and we need to avoid it.

b. **Schedule well**: Don't accept appointments out of fear. Check your schedules to make sure the appointment will fit well into your schedule. Accept an appointment only if you can keep it. It is far better to turn down an appointment than to show up late.

c. **Plan your transport well**: In areas where traffic is not properly organised, it is always important to plan transportation well ahead of time. Set off ahead of schedule to help handle unforeseen circumstances. If necessary, you can use maps to calculate the minimum time required to cover the distance. Then add about 30 minutes to the time to handle unforeseen challenges.

d. **Ask for permission when you are running late**: Sometimes you may still run late even after planning to the best of your ability. When that happens, call immediately to reschedule the meeting. Accept responsibility and apologise for failing to keep the appointment.

e. **Avoid excuses:** Save all your excuses to yourself if you have any, definitely no one is interested. It is your responsibility to keep the schedule because you chose to accept the appointment. If anything goes wrong, even if it is not your fault, you owe an apology for failing to keep the appointment. The reasons why you couldn't keep the appointment is not important.

As children of God, a huge part of our testimony at work depends on how we respect the time of other people. If we are punctual, it affirms our competence. If we show up late to work and meetings, we are stealing time from people and that puts the name of our LORD into disrepute.

Lifelong Learning

Formal education provides an incomplete toolbox and a certificate; lifelong learning is required to use these tools effectively while continuing to equip the toolbox to meet future needs. This makes lifelong education indispensable in the life of every effective worker. Unfortunately, this vital skill is not taught in school.

Lifelong learning is a self-initiated education that is focused on personal development. It refers to all forms of learning that takes places outside the classroom. Lifelong learning involves the ability to identify a knowledge or skill gap, define learning objectives, identify the right sources, patiently master the skill and implement them effectively to solve problems. You may want to study a Character in the Bible, learn to code, pick up some new skills required to solve a problem at work, learn how to handle some basic challenges in your family or learn to write a book. Efficient lifelong learning skills can help you to achieve all these objectives and more.

Lifelong learning requires patience, discipline, and consistency. Patience, because sometimes we don't have enough time to master the skill within a very short period. Mastery of a subject is not achieved in a day. To succeed, we must exercise discipline to stick to our schedules. We must also endure because failure is imminent. Initially, learning can be slow and daunting but if we can persist through the first twenty percent of the work, we often build enough momentum to push through the rest of the learning. Finally, we need to be organized and consistent. We must organise our materials properly and all our notes must be prepared and kept well. If you are organized, you know where to find the right materials for the right job within the shortest possible time. Once consistency is achieved, lifelong learning becomes a habit, less stressful and a rewarding activity. The following plan can help us develop lifelong learning habit:

1. *Define a Project*: Adult learning is daunting when there is no clear reason to learn. Active lifelong learning requires an ambitious project. Why do you want to master this particular skill? Whether the skill is just part of several skills required to solve a major problem or it is a skill needed badly to get you ahead at work, you need to define a project you are passionate about. This will motivate you to overcome the various hurdles.

2. *Define a Fixed Schedule*: A working Schedule is one of the most important prerequisites of lifelong learning. We recommend between 30 minutes and 1 hour of your renewal time at least 4 days in a week. The study time and place should be fixed. You are at liberty to choose what, when and where you want to study but once you have done so, you must stick to your schedule.

3. *Prepare a Learning Contract*: Prepare a learning contract in which you define the purpose or objectives of your study, the learning strategy to adopt, the learning outcomes, proof of learning and

target completion date. Sign the contract to officially commit yourself to the study. The learning contract is meant to define your study path and improve your focus and commitment.

4. *Find an Accountability Partner:* You may need someone you respect to hold you accountable. This person may be your spouse, a brother in Church, a colleague at work or a friend. After you have signed the learning contract, give a copy to your accountability partner and ask him or her to hold you accountable until you have completed the study and achieved the skill. You may also commit to report your progress to your partner on a weekly basis to keep you on track.

5. *Learn one Concept at a Time*: When it comes to knowledge acquisition and skill development, multi-tasking is not a friend. Since we often have less time to master a concept, it is more efficient to concentrate fully on one concept at a time. Big learning goals should be broken down into smaller objectives that can be mastered quickly. If this is done properly, the learner will always be motivated to build on the previously mastered concepts.

First, we should master effective learning skills. Speed reading and comprehension skills, research skills, listening skills, note taking skills, typing skills, design and presentation skills, organization skills, online learning skills and several other concepts that will help us to study efficiently are recommended for a good start. Once these concepts have been mastered, we can learn any concept regardless of the level of difficulty.

How to Rest

One of the most important tasks of the Christian worker is rest. To demonstrate the importance of rest, God rested on the seventh day after creation according to **Genesis 2:2** *"And on the seventh day God ended his work which he had made; and he rested on the seventh day from all his work which he had made"*. Furthermore, Our LORD, Jesus Christ, demonstrated the value of rest in **Mark 6:31** when He said unto His disciples *"...Come ye yourselves apart into a desert place, and rest a while: for there were many coming and going, and they had no leisure so much as to eat"*. This makes rest a very important part of our work life.

Rest is required to restore us physically, emotionally and spiritually after work. As we have read in the previous chapters, the doctrine on work sets high standards and requires that we give everything at work. This means a diligent Christian worker will always come home exhausted. Therefore, a carefully designed rest schedule is required to replenish the lost energy and set us up for the next day's work. A worker who doesn't have an effective rest schedule cannot function consistently at the highest level without burning out. Therefore, it is very important to learn how to rest after work. The following are some suggestions on rest:

1. *Breaks at work are important*: If you work hard, it is fine to enjoy your break time. Use breaks to nourish yourself, rest and bond with colleagues who give positive energy.

2. *Take your bath immediately when you get home*: Head home after work and take your bath first thing when you get home. This will refresh and set you up for your family duties.

3. *Discuss your day with your wife*: Pour out emotional stress and share your challenges with your wife. Talk about your day and listen to how her day went. Your wife will listen and enjoy the conversation if you give her a helping hand in the kitchen or attend to the children. This sets the right tone for a good evening.

4. *Play with your children*: Playing with children can be fun and probably one of the effective ways to laugh and release emotional stress.

5. *Read your Bible and sing the hymns*: Reading scripture and singing sacred music and spiritual songs can lift the spirit. Avoid worldly music.

6. *Have a good bed rest*: This includes at least 6 hours of sleep and a good physical relationship with your wife where possible. There is no better way to rest than this.

7. *Use weekends to recover*: Capitalize on every leisure time during weekends to rest and recover. Sunday afternoons after Church may present good opportunity to get some extra rest.

Avoid worldly forms of leisure such as hanging out with friends to drink. Abstain from all appearance of evil (**1 Thessalonians 5:22**). Worldly forms of leisure may provide temporary relief but the consequences of sin could be devastating. It is also a sin (theft) to use work time for leisure. We must work hard and rest when it is time to do so. Another refreshing habit is prayer. When you feel stressed, it is time to talk to the LORD and lay all burdens at His feet

(**1 Peter 5:7**). He will listen, for He has promised in **Matthew 11:28** *"Come unto me, all ye that labour and are heavy laden, and I will give you rest"*.

Summary

Every fulfilling career is preceded by a deliberate, careful and proper preparation. The believer is required by God to hold high standards at work. It is important to put in the right mechanisms required to function effectively and consistently at the highest level. Everything can be learned. We must learn how to acquire a skill, find a job and manage time to work effectively without compromising our family and Church duties. We must also learn how to rest well so that we can continue to function effectively without burning out. These are the basic building blocks for a successful career. The LORD has made provisions for us to know His will concerning all these things.

GETTING AHEAD AT WORK

"If ye know these things, happy are ye if ye do them" **John 13:17**

The ultimate goal of the believer in the workplace is to be used by God. We haven't lost sight of this. We also believe that our promotion comes only from the LORD (**Psalm 75:6-7**). However, our God is not a rewarder of mediocrity. Therefore, we must aspire to grow in our workplaces.

For a believer, getting ahead at work is not necessarily the same as getting promoted. It doesn't necessarily mean advancing in remuneration and power. Getting ahead at work means increasing our productivity and influence. It means manifesting the excellence of God in our work. We work to get ahead so that we can earn more opportunities to be used by God to influence more lives in our workplaces. That is our motivation. To become exceptionally good at what we do, we must master certain universal skills. Some of these skills are outlined and discussed in this section.

Problem-Solving

Every worker is hired and paid to solve problems. The kind of problem one is hired to address may differ, depending on the work. The mason is hired to build a house according to a designed plan. The teacher is hired to teach students to attain a certain level of competence in a subject area. The doctor is hired to attend to the health of people. Thus, no matter what you do, learning to solve problems effectively is one of the most important skills required to get ahead at work. As a believer, what should be your criteria for solving problems?

1. *Godliness*: the solution we propose to problems must be first and foremost blameless and harmless **(Philippians 2:15)**. Our work must not conflict with the Word of God. The process of implementation, outcomes and the long-term consequences of our solutions must not cause any harm.

2. *Effectiveness*: The proposed solution must be effective. This means the solution should give the desired or promised outcome. We must aim to exceed the expectations of the client.

3. *Timeliness*: The proposed solution must solve the problem on time. The schedule is often defined by

the client in the form of a set deadline. An efficient solution that does not respect the timelines of the client is not good enough. If a client needs a warehouse within six months, the contractor must be able to deliver within six months because every late delivery comes with extra cost to the client.

4. *Efficiency*: The proposed solution must use the available resources efficiently to deliver the desired outcomes. For example, a doctor who prescribes more drugs than required to treat a case is not managing the available resources of the client efficiently. In solving a problem, the available resources must be used wisely to return value for money.

5. *Cleanliness*: the proposed solution must be environmentally friendly. The LORD created a beautiful and sustainable earth. It is our duty to keep it the way it was delivered to us.

Problem-solving is the art and science of mastering how to achieve these objectives. There are several problem-solving frameworks. The reader is strongly encouraged to review some of these frameworks from appropriate sources and master their applications. The following general process is recommended for tackling problems:

1. ***Identify the root cause of the problem***: Every problem has a root cause. Many times, what we see are just the symptoms of a major underlying problem. A lot of effort should be dedicated to unravel the root cause of the problem. For most problems, identifying the root cause constitutes more than 60% of the problem-solving process.

2. ***Find a working solution***: Once the root cause is identified, list all potential solutions to the problem. Then, use the five objectives listed earlier as criteria to test each solution. By subjecting each solution to a rigorous test, most of the proposed solutions will be eliminated leaving a few for implementation.

3. ***Implement the solution***: Implement the solution as soon as possible, get feedback and iterate. Very often, the first solution we propose to a problem may not work to perfection. The feedback obtained after implementation must be used to continually improve the solution until a more plausible solution is obtained. An efficient feedback system can help to improve the solution.

Problem-solving is at the heart of every vocation. Talent and diligence are important but mastery of problem-solving skills in addition to these qualities will produce unmatched efficiency and consistency required to function at the highest level. It is important to note that problem-solving skills are mere tools that cannot replace the need for proper training in one's area of specialization.

Learning on the Job

Every workplace is different. Regardless of your past work experience, some learning on the job would be needed to adapt to the culture, work and life of a new workplace. Your short-term and long-term success would depend to a large extent on your ability to learn fast on the job. There are many technical and non-technical things to learn on the job. Some of the non-technical areas we might need to learn on the job quickly include:

1. *The history of the company*: Learn about the history of the company, its founders, the values on which it was established, its mission, vision and the major milestones of the company. To identify with the vision of the company, you need to know its history. It is also important to know some of the past management members of the company. This gives

you an idea about the kind of skills and attitude you need to get ahead in the company. Finally, learn about how your position became vacant prior to your employment so that you can avoid the mistakes of those who occupied the position previously and learn to fulfil its mandate successfully.

2. *How the company works*: Learn about how the company works, its management structure, its main clients, allies, values, mode of execution, remuneration, challenges, competitors, and other important structures. Make a conscious effort to tour the various departments and familiarize yourself with every department, from security to management. This will help you to move around the company freely, understand why certain tasks are required and work seamlessly with the various structures.

3. *What your boss wants*: Your immediate boss is probably the most important person in the company you need to know. Learn about who he is, his credentials, achievements, work experience, family life, his likes and dislikes, personality and character and above all what he wants from you. Ask him what you can do to make his work efficient and more

enjoyable because your success depends on it. Learn to understand his communication and exactly how he wants his work done. Your main task is to make your boss successful and you can't accomplish it until you know exactly what he wants.

4. ***Key performance indicators***: Every position comes with key performance indicators (KPIs) for evaluating the performance of workers. Learn about all the KPIs associated with your current position, print them out and post a copy in your office where you can see it every day. Keep a copy in your promotional documents file. Knowing the KPIs motivates you to work towards your promotion.

5. ***Everything you can know about your colleagues***: If you work with people, you need to know them. Learn about their habits, personality and character, background and training, how they work, their communication, weaknesses, and strengths. If you know who they are, you can learn to work well with them, help them to overcome their weaknesses and maximize their strengths. Building people up is part of our job as believers in the workplace.

6. ***Where you can find advice and help***: Finally, you need a mentor in the company, a strong character who can hold you responsible, someone you can look up to. That person may not necessarily be a worker in your company but he should have the integrity to advise and guide you through your career.

Technically, it is assumed that you are qualified to hold the position and that is why the company hired you in the first place. However, regardless of your training and work experience, you might need additional tuning to fit into your current job. Humble yourself and be teachable enough to learn from your boss, colleagues and especially those who work under you. As a lifelong learner, complacency and pride should be treated with all contempt. In difficult times, you may also want to consult your external network for wise counsel and technical advice.

Now, the question is how do you learn all these things as fast as possible? We suggest you prepare an outline of all the things you want to learn, in the form of questions in a notebook or on your computer and update the list as you find answers to the questions. This gives you a sense of direction and serves as motivation to be on the lookout for learning opportunities on the job. By doing so, you may find answers to all the important questions and document them for future reference.

Initially, you can find valuable information from the company website, adverts, annual reports, blogs, documentaries, social media handles, social media profiles of workers, inhouse handouts and training platforms. Additional information may be obtained through questioning. If you ask the right people the right questions, you can extract very valuable information. Develop strong networks in the company as soon as possible. Spend lunch breaks with your colleagues, invite them to social events and use every opportunity to ask questions and learn something from them. Finally, do a lot of voluntary jobs for your boss, especially those that can help you to spend more time with him. Some simple tasks such as walking him to the car, meeting him at the car park to help carry a few things, helping to organize his office etc. may go a long way to enhance your relationship and increase your learning opportunities. Use every opportunity to learn something on the job.

Working Hard and Working Smart

Hard work is very rewarding. Unfortunately, many workers don't understand the principles of hard work. Being busy at work doesn't necessarily mean you are working hard. In **2 Thessalonians 3:11**, Paul the Apostle identified some believers who were just **"busybodies"** *"For we hear that there are some which walk among you disorderly, working not at all, but are busybodies"*. Punctuality is a great virtue, but going to work early and leaving work late doesn't equate to working hard. Hard work should be measured in terms of productivity. We have worked hard when our productivity exceeds expectations and we accomplish more tasks than the average worker in the same position. It means giving everything.

People who misunderstand hard work tend to prefer the term "smart work" or "working smart". However, there is not so much difference between working hard and working smart. Working smart often refers to using digital tools or emerging technology to increase productivity. Digital tools have come to stay and they make work easier and faster. Digital tools in the hands of a hardworking man leads to more productivity but the converse is not necessarily true. Working smart or using digital tools cannot change a lazy man into a hardworking man. It is important to understand the difference between working hard and working smart. Hard work is a character that can be enhanced when we learn to work smart. The following suggestions are recommended to help us work hard:

1. *Commit your work to God*: In **Proverbs 16:3** we read *"Commit thy works unto the Lord, and thy thoughts shall be established"*. Let the LORD take absolute control of your work and He will help you to achieve great things. Be filled and led by the Holy Spirit.

2. *Endure it*: As the name suggests, hard work is hard and exhausting, physically, mentally and sometimes emotionally. Very often you might want to simply give up. But know who you are working for and what is at stake. We are called to be hard workers and our master is a rewarder of those who work diligently. If we train ourselves to endure, we can develop a valuable attitude of hard work.

3. *Set targets*: Set monthly, weekly and daily goals to help you focus. Prepare a to-do list before work and discipline yourself to follow your tasks through.

4. *Plan before execution*: For every task, prepare a meticulous plan to get the job done. Planning may take time but if it is done properly, it saves a lot of time in the end.

5. *Master digital tools*: Master existing digital tools and learn to use the right technology for the right job. For every new task, first try to find the right tools to get the job done faster. However, we shouldn't use digital tools for the sake of it. Use technology that is familiar to your boss and accepted by your company.

Hard work is a commendable character. God doesn't approve of slothfulness and mediocrity in any form. The LORD requires our best and it is only by hard work that we can attain such standards.

Managing your Network

Keeping a strong network is one of the most important assets of every worker. A strong network can help our growth and development, help us to share ideas, solve problems and increase accessibility to information in our area of expertise. However, networking can also become distractive if it is poorly built and managed. The following are few ideas to help us manage our networks effectively:

1. **Be open to a wide network**: Build a large network base because every individual you meet is important to the LORD. Not all the people in your network will contribute to your professional growth but

everyone the LORD brings in your way is purposeful. Don't turn down the opportunity to connect with people from different backgrounds and professions. Use every opportunity to connect with people.

2. **Develop a strong core:** Although everyone in your network is important, those who can contribute directly to your professional growth should be kept closer. Build a core network of people you want to grow your profession with. Define the kind of people you want in your core network, search for them and ask them to connect with you. Keep in touch with them, offer help to them when they need it and ask them for help when you are in need. Meet up with them if possible and find ways to share ideas, grow and solve problems together.

3. **Build around mutual interests:** People in your core network should share a common interest with you because strong friendships thrive on mutual goals. Always strive to Keep your relationships professional around something that is of value to all of you. Don't associate with people with questionable character.

4. **Use digital tools to keep in touch:** Digital tools such as LinkedIn, ResearchGate, emails, forums and other professional social media platforms can help you to find people who share a common interest. These applications also offer means to keep in touch with your network.

In a nutshell, networking is all about finding people who share a common interest for the purpose of helping one another grow professionally. As Christian workers, our ideal close associates should be believers who love the LORD and are actively serving Him in their workplaces. This is where Christian men fellowships can be of help if they are built on the right principles and doctrine. Grow and pay attention to your network.

Getting Promoted

Our promotion comes solely from God as we read in **Psalm 75:6-7** *"For promotion cometh neither from the east, nor from the west, nor from the south. But God is the judge: he putteth down one, and setteth up another"*. Therefore, we are not going to teach you some special worldly strategies to scheme your way to the top or push people around to force a promotion. That is ungodly.

Although promotion comes from the LORD, we have a role to play. We need to prepare ourselves to meet all the requirements for godly promotion (**Proverbs 21:31**) because the LORD promotes those who are ready for the next step. The following are required for godly promotion:

1. **Fulfil your current position**: The LORD placed you in your current position for a purpose. Find that purpose and fulfil it. You are not ready for promotion until you have fulfilled your current position. Physically, this means that you need to have fully executed the task you were hired to accomplish, master all the skills required for your next position and aced all the KPIs. Spiritually, you should be used by God to make the right influence in your current position. If you've achieved these things in your current position, then you are ready for the next step.

2. **Inform your boss**: Inform your boss about your intention to apply for promotion because he is the first person to evaluate your application. If he supports your application, chances are that you may sail through. If he doesn't support your application, and the reasons are genuine, you might want to reconsider your application. However, if he opposes

your application on grounds of fear, hatred or jealousy, and you believe strongly that you have fulfilled the position and you are ready for the next step, then go ahead and apply, trusting the LORD who promotes us.

3. **Prepare yourself to apply:** In many institutions, you can apply for promotion when you meet certain conditions. From the first day of work, you can start preparing for the next position. Keep record of all vital documents, reports, achievements, qualifications and other items required to apply for evaluation and promotion.

4. **Apply right:** Meet all requirements and if possible, exceed the minimum requirement for promotion. Prepare all the required documents and apply on time. Make yourself available and get ready for all interviews and evaluations. Then, leave the rest in the hands of the LORD.

5. **Be ready to accept the will of God:** Prepare to accept the will of God, whether it goes your way or not. Promotion comes from the LORD. If He decides that, although you have met all the requirements for promotion but He wants you in your current

position, let His will be done. Don't rebel against the will of God and attempt to scheme your way through because there is nothing good outside the will of God for the believer.

Godly promotion is good and often comes with new challenges and opportunities. However, until you have fulfilled your current position and developed enough skills for the next position, you are not ready to be promoted by God. The most dangerous thing a believer can do is to scheme his way to the top. Prepare yourself for promotion and also prepare to accept the will of God.

When to Find a New Job

It is becoming increasingly likely that a lot of workers will move between jobs in the future. As the way we work changes, many positions will become obsolete and many companies will collapse. It is no longer the norm that one will spend his entire working-life in the same workplace. When is the right time to find a new job? We provide various reasons to find a new job:

1. **When the LORD leads that way:** Sometimes the LORD may lead us into another workplace where He needs us. By no fault of ours, He may bring us

into so much need that the salary of our current work will be unable to meet. By no fault of ours, we may be expelled from our workplace or laid off. In some cases, we may be offered a job in another company through only divinely possible means. When the LORD is working in these directions, probably it is time to move into a new job.

2. **When we are always pushed to sin against God:** If the demands of your current work constantly expose you to acts of corruption, perversion and other forms of sin, it is time to quit and search for a new job. We are commanded to abstain from all appearances of evil. If your job requires you to work on Sundays and keeps you away from serving God or keeps you so busy that you are unable to make time for your family, it is time to move on.

3. **When there is no clear path of development:** If you have outgrown your current position but you don't have any option to get ahead, probably you might want to move to another company where you can grow. Life is lived moving forward and the LORD is not a God of retrogression. He wants us to grow spiritually, physically and professionally.

4. **When your boss just wants you out at all costs:** If you have worked hard and honoured your boss, but somehow he is working around the clock to get you out, probably because of your religion or integrity, maybe you might want to move away if the LORD opens another door. If your presence will cause a problem to many people, sometimes it is better to move away after you have given everything to keep a strong testimony. Do not compromise.

5. **When you lose your job:** If you have lost your job for whatever reason, you need to find another job. If you have served the LORD faithfully in your previous job, you can be very SURE that He will definitely provide another job. He is a faithful God.

It is not easy to move between jobs; good jobs are very scarce. It is therefore, very important to make sure that the LORD approves your switch. Sometimes you have the luxury to find a new job before quitting your job. Many other times, especially when it involves situations that interfere with your relationship with God and your family, you may have to trust the LORD and quit right away. In all, be led by the LORD and seek counsel from people in harmony with the Word of God.

Witnessing at Work

Witnessing at work is the most important task of the believer. Winning souls is at the very top of our priority list. However, with the world becoming increasingly hostile to the Word of God, we need to learn how to achieve this all-important goal without offending people. We must understand that salvation is not the work of man but the Holy Spirit. Our task is to share the Gospel but it is the Holy Spirit who convicts sinners to repentance. Therefore, we must pray and be filled by the Holy Spirit prior to work every day if we want to succeed in soul winning. Pray constantly for your colleagues and ask the LORD to open doors for you to share the Gospel at work. Concentrate on one person at a time. Find your first target, pray for him always and work for opportunities to share the Gospel with him until he understands it well enough to make a decision. If he decides to believe the truth, go ahead and disciple him until he can also witness to other people. If he rejects the truth, remain a good friend, and pray for the next person who is searching for truth. Christ died for all but not everyone will accept Him as Saviour. That is the sad truth. In parts of the world where the Church has already been corrupted and polluted by all manner of pagan teachings, confused doctrines and false gospels, only people who are genuinely searching for truth will accept and believe the Gospel. Don't take offense, rejections are very normal and fine.

First, it is worth repeating that our attitude and output at work is the first preaching that our co-workers will hear. Strive to be perfect in attitude and output at work because every diligent worker will get attention at work. If your attitude, values and work output are exceptional, people will ask questions about your source of motivation. It is almost impossible for a mediocre worker to win souls at work effectively.

Second, don't witness during working hours. Don't turn working hours into preaching time, it shows that you are not serious with your work. The Bible teaches that there is time for everything. As the name suggests, working hours are meant for working and work itself can be your most powerful witnessing tool.

Third, keep the right relationships at work. You cannot preach to your co-workers if you have refused to help them in their time of need. You can't preach to your colleague if you've joined him to gossip about other workers. You can't preach to your co-worker if you discuss profane things with him. You become an effective soul winner at work if you keep a professional and godly relationship with your co-workers.

Fourth, share your testimony. Every Christian came to Christ in a unique and interesting way. We came to Christ from different places, with different stories, but all through the same blood. People, regardless of their religion are interested in stories. Use your first encounter to share your testimony about how you came to Christ and the works He has done in your life. These stories have been used by God on many occasions to inspire interest in people for the Gospel. Once they give attention to the Gospel, you can then preach the Word, which the Holy Spirit uses to bring people to repentance and salvation.

Finally, use free time to share the Gospel or initiate a discussion about the LORD. Share the Gospel with colleagues during breaktime, lunch and after work. Invite them to social events at Church, Church services and Bible studies if necessary. Eat together if that will provide opportunities to share the Gospel. Offer to help them if they need help at work and in their private life or in their homes if that will give an opportunity to share the Word of God. We are servants and servants serve.

Overcoming Trials and Temptations at Work

1 Corinthians 10:13 reads *"There hath no temptation taken you but such as is common to man: but God is faithful, who will not suffer you to be tempted above that ye are able; but will with the temptation also make a way to escape, that ye may be able to bear it"*. Temptations are common in the workplace. We are constantly tempted to steal, lie, pervert and involve ourselves in filthy acts and communications. Fortunately, God always protects us from being tempted beyond our abilities. The LORD always provides a way to escape but it is left to us to identify the way to escape and use it.

In **James 1:13-16** we read that *"Let no man say when he is tempted, I am tempted of God: for God cannot be tempted with evil, neither tempteth he any man: But every man is tempted, when he is drawn away of his own lust, and enticed. Then when lust hath conceived, it bringeth forth sin: and sin, when it is finished, bringeth forth death. Do not err, my beloved brethren"*. The scripture we want to concentrate on is *"**But every man is tempted, when he is drawn away of his own lust, and enticed**"*. From this scripture, the key to preventing temptations is to avoid lust. The cause of every temptation is when we are enticed by our own lust. Consider the temptation to commit sexual sin. If a man has already conceived the thought of taking the lady to bed and actually went ahead to commit the act in his heart, he will be tempted if she entices him by say exposing parts of her body. In this case, the best way to prevent such temptation is for the man to simply discard the thought before it is conceived. How can we deal with lust and temptations in our workplaces?

1. **Pray against Temptations: In Matthew 6:13** the LORD taught us to pray *"And lead us not into temptation, but deliver us from evil: For thine is the kingdom, and the power, and the glory, for ever. Amen"*. Before you go to work, always pray against temptations and be constantly filled with the Holy Spirit. The LORD will protect us from temptations if we ask Him. If He allows us to be tempted after we have prayed against it, He will give us strength to handle it.

2. **Keep your thoughts pure: In Philippians 4:8** we read that *"Finally, brethren, whatsoever things are true, whatsoever things are honest, whatsoever things are just, whatsoever things are pure, whatsoever things are lovely, whatsoever things are of good report; if there be any virtue, and if there be any praise, think on these things"*. As a man thinks, so is he (**Proverbs 23:7**). If your

thoughts are pure, you will be pure and if you keep lustful thoughts, you will eventually fall for it.

3. **Renew your mind:** We read in **Romans 12:2** *"And be not conformed to this world: but be ye transformed by the renewing of your mind, that ye may prove what is that good, and acceptable, and perfect, will of God"*. Lust is a worldly desire and the best way to stand against conforming to the world is by filling our thoughts with the Word of God. Constantly renewing the mind and refocusing on the things of God will keep us away from being enticed by lustful things.

4. **Stay away from all appearance of evil:** In **1 Thessalonians 5:22** we read *"Abstain from all appearance of evil"*. Don't put yourself into a compromising position in your workplace. Don't go to places or put yourself in a position where you will be tempted. Avoid bad friends.

5. **Learn to say no:** Learn to say NO when you find yourself in a tempting position. Don't fear how the people involved may feel, just learn to do right by saying no politely. You are a child of God, don't allow people to push you out of the will of God.

6. **Trust the LORD with your job:** Many times, workers yield to temptations because of fear of losing their jobs. If you believe that you were placed in the workplace by the LORD for His purpose, then you don't need to be afraid of being sacked from your job. Stand firm and do what is right and when you are pushed to the wall, be courageous and quit. The LORD is faithful to provide another job.

Trials and temptations will come. We get tempted if we first lust after the thing which tempts us. The LORD protects us from falling for these temptations by providing a way to escape. Let us exercise ourselves to avoid lust in our workplaces, pray constantly and learn to use the way to escape when you are tempted.

Building People at Work

We read in **Romans 15:1** "*We then that are strong ought to bear the infirmities of the weak, and not to please ourselves*" and **Galatians 6:2** reads "*Bear ye one another's burdens, and so fulfil the law of Christ*". Good workers build their co-workers. The success of a leader is in his ability to develop a successor. We must learn to build co-workers because it makes us more efficient. It enables us to delegate some of our tasks and find help from people we can trust. Building people at work also empowers them to build others, creating a community of efficient workers. Also, empowering people creates an environment where workers support one another. Finally, building people around us gives us more opportunities to share our testimony as believers and ultimately find more opportunities to witness for the LORD.

The believer should not be afraid to empower people at work. Most workers are afraid of building people around them in an attempt to protect their position. Some would not empower workers for fear of losing their relevance. People have various reasons, including fear of betrayal, ingratitude, among other reasons. However, the believer must not be afraid of lifting the weak because he works for the LORD and his position is kept by God. To empower people at work, the following are recommended:

1. **Train one person at a time:** Training is efficient when it is personalised. Identify a worker who is teachable and concentrate your time and resources on him. The training offered should be in such a way that the trainee is trained to train others. Empowering too many people at a time is difficult and often does not produce the kind of efficiency required for high-level performance.

2. **Demonstrate genuine love and care:** Workers would feel comfortable and readily learn from people they can trust. If you can show true love and care for your workers, they will always run to you for help and teaching.

3. **Avoid micro-management:** You are training workers to develop themselves. It is not good to micro-manage them or try to tell them what to do and insist that they do things your way always. That may stifle innovation and growth. Give freedom for trainees to choose what they want to learn and how they want to develop themselves. Yours is to support and direct their development.

4. **Be ready to answer questions:** Workers will learn from colleagues who listens to their questions and helps them find meaningful answers. Always prepare to answer questions and give attention to workers who want to learn. Be ready to communicate and teach those who show interest in learning.

5. **Patience, Patience and more Patience:** Many workers are slow learners. They don't lack the ability to learn, they are only slow and sometimes understand things differently. A lot of patience may

be required to guide and encourage them along the way. Workers who are slow to learn often learn better in the long term. Be patient.

The secret to empowering people at work is to be a good learner. If we give ourselves to learning, we position ourselves to help those who are in need of knowledge and guidance. Don't be afraid of building people at work because it honours God.

Leading for God at Work

Leadership is one of the most discussed subjects in recent times due to its importance in the corporate world. In the previous chapter, we discussed some of the important qualities of a leader, using Nehemiah as a case study. Leaders in the workplace are very important to the Great Commission due to the opportunities and influence such positions present for soul-winning. A lot of exhaustive books have been written on this subject. The reader is encouraged to read a lot on leadership, especially books in harmony with scripture. In this section, we discuss an important leadership principle that is often neglected or overlooked by many Christian leaders in the workplace.

In **1 Corinthians 11:1** the Apostle Paul said *"Be ye followers of me, even as I also am of Christ"*. In this short scripture lies one of the most powerful leadership principles in the Bible. God has a special plan for all humanity and the whole world. All things were made by Him for His purpose. The people we are called to lead in our workplaces are part of this big plan. You have been appointed by God to lead these people to that place where the LORD wants to take them. That is the sole purpose of leadership, to command and guide a group of people to follow the plan of God. That is why it is impossible to lead successfully for God if we don't know Him. If you don't have a special relationship with the LORD, you wouldn't know His plan for the group you are leading and you can't follow His leading.

Many Christians leading in their workplaces have failed to influence the workplace for God because they have led the people out of the will of God. Some leaders are struggling to impact the workplace for God because they are using worldly principles to lead. God doesn't need a very specialised person to lead in the workplace. He doesn't need people with MBAs in leadership or people who know all the leadership principles to lead in the workplace. What He has required is a man who will fully obey Him and follow His leading. God needs someone who will simply say "follow me as I follow the LORD". This is the central principle of strong godly leadership in the workplace. In summary, a leader who seeks to be used by God must:

1. Be a child of God
2. Know the purpose of God for the group he is leading
3. Be led by God
4. Lead and command the people to follow him as he follows the LORD

This is the ultimate purpose of God for leaders in our workplaces. Leaders who uphold this principle will be successful in their quest to win the workplace for Christ.

Working in a Team

In today's workplace, most important projects are executed by project teams. A team often comprises two or more workers from various backgrounds with different skill sets and work experiences. What makes a team powerful is synergy - the interaction of the individual talents and skills to produce a combined effect greater than the sum of their separate effects. Thus, teamwork is more than individual contributions from two or more workers. How to produce maximum synergy in a team is the subject of this section.

In **Amos 3:3** we are asked *"Can two walk together, except they be agreed?"*. In this scripture is the secret to working successfully in a team. The main reason why many teams struggle to get things done successfully is often because there is no clear agreement between team members. Leaders define a task and assemble a team to execute the task without taking into consideration how to combine the individual strengths of team members to produce maximum synergistic effect while minimising disagreements and internal conflicts. Workers come into a team with various disagreements, attitudinal problems and personal conflicts. If these challenges are not properly managed, the team will fail and a few people or sometimes just one person may end up working on the task.

The first need of a team is to get members to agree and commit to the work. If you agree to distribute tasks among group members, put it in writing and ask team members to sign their commitment to execute the task assigned to them within the stipulated deadline. If you agree on regular meetings to discuss the challenge, prepare a written agreement and ask team members to commit to it. If you agree to collaborate online, do the same. Always make sure there is a clear agreement on how the job is to be done and all team members have agreed and are committed to working according to plan. This brings seriousness and focus to the task.

Second, tasks that are agreed by all teammates should be tackled first. This reduces the efforts, resources and time often wasted on useless debates and arguments. As you focus on the agreed tasks, you build time to think through and resolve all challenges around the disputed tasks. Time, they say heals wounds. By working this way, you may even come to realise that some of the disputed tasks are not important. Don't reject individual contributions simply because the group disagrees. Write down every contribution and suggestion but work on tasks that have the approval of all team members first before you consider the disputed tasks and contributions.

When working in a team, the believer should show himself faithful and commit fully to the work. We should not mind working harder than all team members if that will enhance our testimony. We should disagree politely when conflicting ideas arise and avoid the temptation to involve ourselves in a strife. Avoid filthy jokes and profane language. Don't use working hours for personal discussions. The believer should be peculiar in the team and seen as an indispensable member of the team.

Summary

It is the desire of every worker to advance in his career. In the life of Joseph, we see that God promotes those who put their trust in Him. Although promotion comes from the LORD, we are required to meet certain criteria for promotion. The Christian worker who honours God with his work can trust the faithfulness of God in his work. The Word of God is still very applicable in today's fast-paced workplace. If we truly want to influence the workplace for Christ, we must change the way we work. The LORD has strong principles for those who want to serve Him in their workplaces. It is impossible to please Him with our work if we work contrary to His Word. May the LORD help us to fulfil His purpose for our lives in our workplaces.

FAMILY AND WORK

"Thus saith the LORD, Stand ye in the ways, and see, and ask for the old paths, where is the good way, and walk therein, and ye shall find rest for your souls. But they said, We will not walk therein." **Jeremiah 6:16**

In this chapter, we present a hard Biblical doctrine that has become a controversial subject today. This book is written for matured believers who are in search of the will of God concerning their career and businesses. The doctrine presented here is not meant to change the views of the world or compel everyone to accept the will of God. However, the reader is encouraged to check everything he reads in this book with the Bible, which is the standard of truth. In the first Chapter, we showed from the Bible that our works don't count for salvation. Our redemption was solely paid for by the blood of Jesus Christ. Therefore, the salvation of the believer will not be affected in any way if he refuses to follow the will of God. His fellowship with the LORD will be impaired, not his salvation.

However, the testimony of the believer will be greatly enhanced if he decides to follow this path laid down by the LORD. An enhanced testimony also means that the believer will stand a better chance of being used more by God. We read in **Jeremiah 6:16** that if we walk in the old paths laid down by God, we shall find rest for our souls. God has a perfect plan for everything and his plan was laid down before the foundations of the world. Sometimes, lack of knowledge and fear of men may prevent us from walking fully in the will of God. But we ought to fear and obey God rather than men (**Acts 5:29, Matthew 10:28**). In the will of God is perfect peace and joy. However, our walk with God is a journey and everyone is at a different stage in this journey. We are all striving for perfection but we are still sinners in a sinful world. What the LORD require is an open heart that is searching for His will.

How God Created the Family

God instituted the family with a man and a woman complementing each other to serve Him (**Revelations 4:11**). In simple terms, the family has two important needs; procreation and provision. Procreation involves building a family, receiving and raising children for the LORD. Provision includes feeding, protection and leadership. In His perfect wisdom, God instituted the family with a man and a woman, two equally important but different people, and assigned them these two equally important but different roles. The man is tasked to lead, protect and provide for the family and the woman is assigned to keep the home, raise children and guide the house. This is the perfect plan God instituted to make the family sustainable. The LORD did not assign the man the provisional roles because he is better than the woman and God did not assign the woman the procreational roles because she is better than the man. This has been the only plan for the family, practiced throughout the Bible and through times of old until somewhere after the second world war. This perfect plan works for two reasons. First, God has created the man and woman, each with special potentials to make them successful and fulfilled at their respective tasks. Second, once the role is accepted in obedience to God, He provides special grace to complement our weaknesses so that each can fulfil His will in the assigned roles. The grace of God is always within the will of God.

Family-Work Balance

Procreation and provision are two huge tasks, each requires full attention to meet the perfect will of God. Each of these tasks is a full-time job. The perfect will of God is for the man to work full-time and provide fully for the whole family. The woman is to work full-time at home and see to all the procreational needs of the family. Today, this plan has been distorted. The man is expected to work a full-time job and provide for the family but also take some procreational duties at home. The woman is expected to work full-time job but with no strong obligation to provide for the family while her procreational duties are outsourced to other people who are often paid by the man. There are many variations of this modern plan. Basically, both the man and the woman have belittled and, in some cases, abandoned the procreational duties in competition for the provisional duties. The motivation is for each person to earn his or her own money. Covetousness has led to this distortion. There are several distortions of the family system today. The fact that we have several forms of these distortions means we still haven't found a working plan. Since the inception of these so-called new systems, divorce rate has increased significantly, the family has produced more wayward children, crime has increased, sexual perversion in the workplace has gone up and families have become weaker and so is the Church. These so-called modern family systems don't work because of two reasons. First, because the man and woman are both expected to work outside their comfort zone. Second, because they have abandoned the perfect will of God and working without His grace in the family.

Because the man and woman are somehow involved in both the procreational and provisional duties in an undefined way, the term family-work balance has been devised to provide techniques to help them manage the duties. However, in reality, family-work balance is impossible to achieve because each is a full-time job. Most often, the family is sacrificed to earn more money to pay for the damages caused by abandoning the family. Many people complain that the cost of living is so high that it is impossible for a family to live on a single income stream. That is not true. God has never instituted any plan that gets outdated. His Word always works, every time, everywhere, if implemented according to His well.

Feminism and the Bible

The **Encyclopaedia Britannica** defines Feminism as *"the belief in social, economic, and political equality of the sexes"*. Feminism is not just an idea, it is a "belief" or faith, similar to a religion. In simple terms, it is a cult. According to the feminist faith, men and women are equal, socially, economically and politically. But is this the view of the Bible?

Social equality of the sexes: Social equality suggest that God created the man and woman equally and therefore each can play any role in the family. But according to the Bible, God created the man first and then created the woman as a help meet for him because *"...It is not good that the man should be alone..."* (**Genesis 2:18**). After the man was created, we read in **Genesis 2:22-24** that God took a rib from the man to create the woman. Thus, it is clear that a man and a woman were created differently. The man was not created better than the woman, they were just created different. Additionally, we read in **Genesis 5:2** that *"Male and female created he them..."*. God created two different people, male and female. They are different and things that are different are not the same. In the sight of God, the man is not more important than the woman and the woman is not more important than the man. God created two equally important but different people for different purposes. That is the position of the Bible which is the direct opposite of the social equality aspect of feminism.

Political equality of the sexes: Political equality suggests that the man and the woman should have equal leadership roles in the family. The position of the Bible is that the man is the head of the woman as written in **1 Corinthians 11:3** *"But I* *would have you know, that the head of every man is Christ; and the head of the woman is the man; and the head of Christ is God*". In **Genesis 3:16,** God said to the woman "*You will desire your husband, and he will rule over you*". Again, in **Ephesians 5:23** we read that "*For the husband is the head of the wife, even as Christ is the head of the church: and he is the saviour of the body*". All these scriptures are clear that the man is the head of the woman. In other words, the man is given the responsibility to lead the family and he is accountable to God for everything that happens in the family. This leadership role is not a privilege as the world wrongly interprets it but a huge responsibility. Again, the feminist believe of political equality is in direct conflict with the Word of God.

Economic equality of the sexes: Economic equality suggest that the man and woman should work and be financially independent and contribute equally to provide for the family. This is what most people practice today. But God commands only the man, who is the head of the family, to provide for his home according to **1 Timothy 5:8** "*But if any provide not for his own, and specially for those of his own house, he hath denied the faith, and is worse than an infidel*". In **Genesis 3:19,** God said to the man "*In the sweat of thy face shalt thou eat bread, till thou return unto the ground; for out of it* *wast thou taken: for dust thou art, and unto dust shalt thou return*". Nowhere in the Bible did God command the woman to work and provide for her family. The Bible requires wives "*To be discreet, chaste, **keepers at home**, good, obedient to their own husbands, that the word of God be not blasphemed*" (**Titus 2:5**). This doctrine is repeated in **1 Timothy 5:14** "*I will therefore that the younger women marry, bear children, **guide the house**, give none occasion to the adversary to speak reproachfully*". In **Proverbs 31,** we read about the works of the virtuous woman. A closer look at the works of the virtuous woman shows that almost all the works she is involved daily are mostly done in the home, apart from going out to gather her raw materials. From these scripture, and against popular modernist and feminist stands, it is clear that wives are instructed to stay at home and carry out some important and well-defined tasks. A man and a woman were not meant to be economically equal as it is been pushed around by feminist. It is the sole duty of a man to provide fully for the family, and that includes the needs of his wife. The needs of girls are provided by their father until he hands them over to their husbands in marriage to take over the responsibility.

From this Bible point of view, it is impossible to be a believer and a feminist. If you are a feminist because you didn't know what it stands for, that is pardonable. Biblical Christianity and feminism are two separate and directly opposite faith. Unfortunately, many women have been deceived to believe that the ultimate achievement of a woman is to become a man. That a woman is only successful if she ends up in the role of a man. Many women have wasted their whole life trying to prove that they can play the role of a man. The capability of women has never been in doubt. Although women can execute most of the tasks assigned to men in the workplace, there is nothing that a woman can do in the workplace that a man can't. On the other hand, there are many roles a woman can play at home that a man can never do.

Many women have been deceived into the cult of feminism because they think it "empowers" or "liberate" women. There is no civilization or culture in the history of the world that empowers and liberates women more than the Bible's way. Actually, feminism enslaves women because it puts pressure on them to abandon their God-given tasks and move out of their comfort zones into places where they can't find fulfilment. Every sincere woman would admit that her fulfilment is in her home and children. She may enjoy the money and fame that comes with her work but her ultimate fulfilment is in her home. That is just how God created women. Women are not inferior to men as feminism tries to portray. Men are not the problem of women as feminism tries to teach. Everyone can be successful and fulfilled in the sight of God.

The Three Types of Wives

The modern Bible perversions have removed **"keepers at home"** and **"guide the house"** from **Titus 2:5** and **1 Timothy 5:14,** respectively and replaced them with more liberal and contemporary statements such as *"to be busy at home"* (**NIV**), *"to work in their homes"* (**NLT**), *"homemakers"* (**NKJV**) just to mention a few. It is clear that the same old serpent who approached Eve in the garden of Eden and questioned the Word of God *"Yea, hath God said"* (**Genesis 3:1**) is determined to destroy women with these intentionally twisted translations. What is so important about these scriptures that the devil doesn't want us to know? We shall soon find out. Let us examine the three common types of wives:

1. *The career wife*: this is the most popular and accepted position even in our Baptist Churches today. A wife is expected to keep a full-time or at least a part-time job, work and contribute financially to the family. To

make this possible, children are enrolled in schools as soon as possible, sometimes a nanny or a mother-in-law is engaged to care for the children, a housemaid is employed to keep the house and a teacher is hired to help the children with their homework. In some cases, the husband and wife try to manage some of the duties together to reduce the cost. Sometimes all the duties of the wife except her conjugal duties are delegated or outsourced to other people so that she can pursue a career, work and make money to pay people to execute her duties at home. Some have tried so hard to combine their home duties with their job but that always affects the job of the husband as he need to stand in for her in most of the duties at home. Unfortunately, it has become obsolete to train girls into wives and mothers. Girls are rather trained to become career women who can take on lucrative jobs, work and pay other people to carry out their duties at home. But does this really improve the productivity of the family?

2. *The housewife*: these are wives who have been asked by their husbands to stay at home either because they don't need to work, the husband is afraid to expose his wife to sexual predators in the workplace, to

follow a tradition or for health reasons. The wife has no defined duties at home. At most she is expected to cook and pick the children from school. In some weird cases practiced by some rich people in Africa, all the domestic duties of the wife are outsourced to workers and family folks. The wife is just expected to stay home, relax, shop and keep herself beautiful and attractive for her husband. This encourages laziness.

3. *The "keeper at home" wife*: this is the position of the Bible. The wife is instructed to stay at home and carry out the following God-given duties:

   a. **Keep the home (Titus 2:5, Proverbs 31)**: home-keeping duties include managing the family finances, planning, budgeting and shopping all the needs of the family. It also includes cooking the meals, cleaning, putting the house in order and guiding the house. Applicable skills include resource management, financial accounting, interior decoration, planning, shopping and project management.

   b. **Love their husbands (Titus 1:4)**: this includes loving, honouring and serving the needs of her husband. It also includes taking care of his health needs, keeping him motivated, managing his stress, making sure he is prepared and ready for work, helping him in decision making and helping him in his work by carrying out duties such as typing, filing, research and other simple tasks. Applicable skills include human relations, office skills, stress management, business secretariat and decision analysis.

c. **Love their children (Titus 1:4):** this includes receiving children from God, as many as He provides, caring for all their needs and raising and training them to love the LORD. It includes health needs such as feeding, cleaning and playing. It also includes training, teaching the Word of God, home-schooling them and teaching them to carry out important domestic duties. Girls are trained into wives and mothers and boys are trained into hardworking faithful men and fathers who will love and provide for their families. The goal is to return the children back to God through Christ. The objective is not to train them into rich and famous people, that is not the objective of godly parenting. Godly parents aspire to train children into responsible believers who will love and serve the LORD. Applicable skills include teaching skills, child psychology, strong organisation skills, first aide, conflict resolution and education management.

First, it is impossible to successfully combine these tasks with a full-time job without outsourcing. That is why the Bible instructs wives to be "keepers at home". Second, a woman who is not saved cannot serve the LORD at home in this way. That is why a believer should not be unequally yoked with an unbeliever in marriage. Third, a woman must be properly educated to serve the LORD at home. The duties outlined above with their various skill needs require proper education and lifelong learning to accomplish. Finally, this is not a boring job at all. It is probably the most exciting and challenging job out there that require a lot of learning and diversity of knowledge. The challenge is the humility required to serve your own family with the same sense of urgency, attention and love you would give to other people at a paying job. Unfortunately, women would serve other people at work rather than give the same level of attention and love to their family because our society calls the former "good customer service" and the later "slavery".

The Responsibilities of the Man and Woman

In terms of authority, there are about three family systems; (1) the family where the husband is in charge, (2) the family where the wife is in charge and (3) the family where God is in charge. Recently, another deceptive position is emerging where the home is assumed to be under equal authority of the man and the woman. There is a reason why no company has two CEOs. It is impossible to run a complex institution such as the family under two conflicting authorities. Actually, any time a couple pretend to rule the home together, it is often the woman that is in charge. The third type of family where God is the only authority in the home is the position of the Bible. The LORD who has full authority over the family then assigns duties to the husband and the wife. The husband and wife carry out their various duties in obedience to God unto whom they are both accountable.

1. *Role of the man*: First, it is the responsibility of the man to implement a family structure that is in full harmony with the Word of God. This is his most important and difficult task. He is to ensure that he keeps a family alter to teach his family the Word of God in the morning and evenings before and after work, teach his wife to accept her God-given duties

to stay at home and rule over his home for the LORD in love. The man also works full-time and provides for all the needs of the family – himself, his wife and his children. This enables him to concentrate fully on his work. He doesn't need to worry about domestic duties, except his task to provide, protect, teach and lead his family. He may help his wife to handle some duties at home after work but he is not obliged to do it. That is the man may still be seen taking on some domestic duties sometimes but his wife will not demand that he do them. Rather she appreciates the help lend out by her husband.

2. ***Role of the woman***: The first duty of the wife is to accept her God-given responsibility to serve the LORD at home. A woman who loves God and wants to walk in His ways will easily accept this position. In addition to the responsibilities already discussed, the woman accepts and manages all the finances of the family according to instructions passed on to her by her husband. After tithes and offerings are deducted, she takes out the investment and savings funds into the appropriate accounts, services all debts, pays the bills and manages the rest of the

income to meet the needs of the family. Money should be spent transparently and documented for full accountability to her husband at the end of the month before new income is received. She is to inform her husband about new family needs and upcoming family events and plan towards them. She institutes a school at home with all the necessary syllabi and materials to home-school the children. Thus, the woman and all her children stay at home full-time except when she is out shopping, taking the children out or attending to other needs of the family.

As you may have noticed, this is not a system that can be easily practiced by unbelievers. It requires the commitment and trust of both husband and wife. This level of commitment and trust is only possible when both carry out their responsibilities to honour God under the leadership and guidance of the Holy Spirit.

Comparative Advantage of the Family System

We examine the benefits of the woman staying at home in terms of four key areas; Productivity, Savings, Service to God and Sustainability.

1. ***Productivity***: God provides through only the man. The man is fully focused on his work. He can grow and advance quickly in his career and earn higher income for the family. If his income is insufficient, he is at liberty to take additional jobs as long as it does not interfere with his ability to hold his responsibilities at home. He has enough time to take courses, develop skills and build a strong career. He is also able to take on extra tasks at work to improve his chances of getting promoted. The woman on the other hand is fully concentrated on her domestic duties. She is able to make enough time to study and develop the skills required to manage her tasks efficiently. She can learn to cook new meals, develop routines to keep the home better, and develop several useful skills that will eventually save the family a lot of money. In the case where both partners work for money, they are distracted by domestic duties and have to run between their jobs and the family. They lack the concentration to work effectively and get ahead in their work. Self-development becomes even difficult and in an ideal workplace it is harder for them to advance in their career. Spiritually, because the family is doing the will of God, if the man obeys

the LORD fully in his work according to the doctrine outlined in this book, he will be blessed immensely and get ahead even faster in his career.

2. *Savings*: where the woman is working at home, money is saved through proper planning and wise shopping. She has enough time to plan ahead and search for the right shops and markets where she can buy quality products at affordable prices. Many career women can hardly make time for shopping. They buy online and grab things on their way home. Because the children are at home and eat home-cooked meals, they stay healthy and strong, saving a lot of money on medical bills. We know how many times children bring sicknesses from schools and day-care (or rather don't-care) centres. Home-schooling also reduces the cost of school fees, transportation, security risks and other unnecessary expenses. The man can eat two meals at home and take a packed lunch to work to reduce the cost of eating out while improving his health. Money is saved on nannies, babysitters, housemaids, security men and other expenses such as the need for additional car. Both partners are fully active and engaged in their work, which improves their health

and makes them less susceptible to temptations. All these savings are lost when both partners work. It is not difficult to prove that the amount of money earned by most career women is not even enough to offset all these losses. At face value, it might seem like a loss when the woman works at home but actually it saves a lot of money.

3. ***Service to God***: the man, who is fully focused on his job is able to serve the LORD fully at work and keep a strong testimony through his work output. He has the liberty to develop his skills and become an exceptional worker. He can go soul-winning on Saturdays to share the Gospel with the unsaved and he has time to take additional duties in the Church. The woman, who is fully engaged at home is able to fulfil all her God-given responsibilities at home; keeping the home, loving her husband and her children. She is also able to teach her children the Word of God, train them in the ways of the LORD and trust the LORD to save them (**2 Timothy 3:15**). The family has enough time to hold a family devotion every morning and evenings if they desire. Generally, there is enough peace and less stress to enjoy family life and serve the LORD fully. In the

case where both partners work, every morning, they rush to work and drop the children at school among other things. They hardly have time for prayer. After work, they rush to pick their children, grab a few things in the market and head home. The whole family is tired and can hardly hold an evening prayer. Husband and wife are so stressed they hardly have a peace of mind to serve the LORD cheerfully and many times their physical relationship in the bedroom is a huge challenge. Family life is sacrificed when both partners pursue a career. The children are mainly parented by their teachers at school and other people who expose them to false teachings, strange behaviours and social vices among other security and moral risks.

4. *Sustainability*: in this uncertain world, stability of the family is paramount. The family which is under the authority of God is the most stable family by far. Only the man's job depends on external forces, everything else is done at home. If the country is shut-down and schools and even Churches are closed down, the family will still run normal as long as the man can go to work. The family can easily move to another city if they decided to take on a new job,

serve the LORD in a new capacity or the man is transferred from his work. No extended family members, nanny or maid is needed to run the home. The husband and wife are able to take care of all the responsibilities of the family without any external help. Only the man is exposed to external security risks and that is how it should be because the man is commanded to love his family the same way Christ loved and died for the Church. There is a dedicated person for managing the finances of the family. This enables money to be used wisely, saved and invested to earn more income. The children are parented fully according to Biblical doctrine, giving them a good chance of getting saved and becoming active believers. Well-parented children will grow up into responsible and wise adults who will not destroy the properties of the family. The husband and wife enjoy a close relationship, reducing the chances of separation. The family has room to accept any number of children from the LORD because this system works very well for even large families.

Women who have accepted this role looks younger, healthier, happier and more fulfilled. It comes with far less challenges compared to pursuing a career. The challenges of a full-time job include stress, sexual harassment, confusion, useless competitions, worry, disrespect, bad marriage, unparented children, and emptiness. Every godly husband loves a woman who keeps her home and most responsible men will readily give anything for their wives to accept this role. On the other hand, a man who is loved by his wife this way has no reason to look elsewhere for anything. He is healthier, happier and lives longer. Most men die young because of stress and frustration.

Peculiar African Challenges

This Biblical family system is fairly new in Africa as many consider it alien to our culture. But this is the oldest family system and the closest to the Bible. The Word of God is profitable to every people who would simply obey the LORD. African believers who have practiced this system have found that it works. My wife and I learned this system from a missionary who had really beautiful, amazingly lovely and unnaturally happy family. We have practiced this system for about eight years and the results are great. We know a few other Ghanaian Baptists who have taken this old path. In this section, we attempt to address some of the main challenges we've found.

1. ***The Extended Family System***: In Africa, most ethnic groups practice the extended family system. Marriage is seen as a union of two families rather than a man and a woman. Thus, the family consist of a man, woman, children and the family members of the man and the woman. The man and the woman owe their respective families financial support in times of need. In some cases, family members, especially parents depend fully on the financial support of their children during old age due to bad social security. This brings high financial pressure on the family and a genuine reason for women to pursue a career. However, Biblical wisdom can handle this challenge. First, part of the family savings should be used to provide for extended family needs. However, the best way to support extended family folk is to invest for them. Family members who can work should never be given money directly but rather an investment where they can put in some work to earn their daily living. We must always enforce discipline to ensure that family dependants learn to use money wisely. It is the responsibility of the man to ensure that extended family dependants are taken care of properly.

2. *Social Security*: Social security is a major challenge in Africa. Women may be afraid to serve the LORD at home if sufficient provision is not made for their social security. To handle this challenge, first, the woman who works at home must be made the next of kin of all investment and financial documentations. She must be given 100% entitlement to all family properties, which means that her name should be included in the documents of all family properties. Second, a private social security fund should be created for her. This will insure her sufficiently for the future. However, our security is in the LORD and those who obey Him shall never be disappointed (**Romans 10:11**).

3. *Divorce and Remarriage*: As Independent Baptist, divorce is an abomination. It is not an option for us because it is against scripture. God hates divorce. However, many women are afraid that their husbands might change their minds and so they need to prepare sufficiently for divorce. I have found that women who prepare for divorce often get divorced. For a true believer, divorce is not something that just happen. The first reason why many get divorced is because they make it an option. The other causes of

divorce are sex, money and children. This family system is less susceptible to divorce because it handles these three problems far better than any modern system. Husband and wife live together and are always available for sex. The children are parented according to scripture and this system has a clear plan for earning and using money in the family, avoiding most of the disagreements.

4. *Life Expectancy*: Life expectancy in Africa is very low. Many women might be afraid that their husbands may die early and leave them alone with many children to cater for. But who is the preserver and taker of life? God is the giver and taker of life. First, if the man and woman serve and trust the LORD fully, He will take care of these things. Second, many men die in Africa because of stress and sin. Men who love their jobs and have peace in their homes are less likely to die young. Men who eat healthy meals at home and walk in peace with God are more likely to live longer. But yet again there is no regret in obeying God, He knows and cares about our needs. In **1 Kings 3:14**, the LORD promised to lengthen the days of King Solomon if he walks in His ways. There is length of days and long life in obeying God.

5. *Inheritance*: Inheritance of properties after the demise of the man can be a complicated issue. Proper planning and anticipation can handle this challenge. ALL properties must be fully willed to the woman. Extended family dependants should be educated. Those who are lazy should be disciplined by cutting financial support. The hardworking dependants should be supported sufficiently to uplift them.

6. ***Pressure to pursue a career***: There is always social, economic and political pressure on women to pursue a career. We don't condemn humble and obedient Christian women who have been pushed by their husbands, extended family and other stakeholders to pursue a career as long as they understand the position of the Bible. No man is perfect. Proper education and wise counsel can help a woman who is a believer to stay on course for the LORD. Many women are under pressure to work career jobs because their husbands have refused to take full responsibility of the family. The man must provide fully. Some are pursuing career because they have been misinformed that staying at home means they are sacrificing their godly calling to serve society.

There is no better way a woman can serve society than to stay at home, keep the home and raise well taught and responsible children for society. However, believers don't live to serve society; our desire is to serve our God. Most career women are driven by money, fame and competition. Our focus is on eternity, we are not interested in dominating the world, becoming rich and famous people. Proper Biblical education and wise counsel can help many women understand and enjoy their position.

Summary

The family as instituted by God in the Bible is very sustainable. The family instituted by God mandates the man to work and provide fully for the family while the woman works at home to keep the home, love her husband and raise children for the LORD. We have shown that such a family is more robust than the case where both the man and the woman pursue a career and financial independence. We also believe that this old way is still the best way in terms of productivity, stability and financial freedom. Proper training is required to institute this family system. My wife, Susan, and I are open to sharing our experiences with families who see this as an option.